# BENJAMIN B. WARFIELD AND RIGHT REASON

## *The Clarity of General Revelation and Function of Apologetics*

Owen Anderson

University Press of America,® Inc.
Lanham · Boulder · New York · Toronto · Oxford

Copyright © 2005 by
University Press of America,® Inc.
4501 Forbes Boulevard
Suite 200
Lanham, Maryland 20706
UPA Acquisitions Department (301) 459-3366

PO Box 317
Oxford
OX2 9RU, UK

All rights reserved
Printed in the United States of America
British Library Cataloging in Publication Information Available

Library of Congress Control Number: 2005931896
ISBN 0-7618-3288-2 (paperback : alk. ppr.)
ISBN: 978-0-7618-3288-1

The paper used in this publication meets the minimum
requirements of American National Standard for Information
Sciences—Permanence of Paper for Printed Library Materials,
ANSI Z39.48—1984

Contents:

Foreword                                                          v

Introduction
xxiii

Chapter 1: Princeton Theological Seminary and Common Sense
Philosophy                                                        1

Chapter 2
Benjamin B. Warfield and Right Reason: The Clarity of General
Revelation and Function of Apologetics                           15

Chapter 3
Benjamin B. Warfield and Abraham Kuyper: Worldview
Relativism and the Question of First Principles
            23

Chapter 4
Benjamin B. Warfield and Cornelius VanTil: Westminster
Theological Seminary and the Presuppositional Apologetics of
Cornelius VanTil                                                 45

Conclusion                                                       63

# Foreword:
# On The Necessity For Natural Theology

Owen Anderson has ably analyzed the epistemology of B.B. Warfield in contrast to that of Abraham Kuyper and Cornelius VanTil. He has done this in order to draw attention to the necessity of clarity and inexcusability if the claims of historic Christian theism are to be meaningfully understood. Any thoughtful Christian apologetic must therefore begin with showing the clarity of general revelation in order to establish the inexcusability of unbelief.

In philosophy, this intellectual endeavor has been the domain of natural theology. Mr. Anderson's analysis of Warfield has therefore shown the necessity for the project of natural theology. But what would be required to undertake this project? The next stage in the project, prior to the actual execution of the project, is to sketch the program of natural theology. What are the general objections to natural theology which must be met, and what is the scope and sequence of the proofs required in showing clarity and inexcusability?

Natural theology attempts to show what can be known of God and man and good and evil from general revelation. Skepticism in general maintains knowledge is not possible hence natural theology is not possible. Fideism in general maintains that proof for one's first principles is not necessary hence natural theology is not necessary. Before engaging in its program natural theology (NT) must show why proof is necessary and how knowledge is possible. The possibility, necessity, and extent of the knowledge of God become more evident in historic Christian theism which is based on the over-arching and under-girding themes of creation, fall, and redemption.

# I
## Skepticism

In the history of skepticism, from ancient to contemporary, the basis of skepticism has shifted. At times it is grounded metaphysically in various formulations of the problem of the one and the many. At other times it is grounded epistemologically in variations of empiricism and rationalism. Most recently it has been grounded in hermeneutics, in issues related to interpreting experience and constructing worldviews. From time to time it has been grounded in the nature of knowledge itself, whether knowledge is discursive, cognitive, and propositional, or whether it is relational, mystical, and a matter of encounter.

Metaphysical skepticism denies there is an object of knowledge. In the ancient world this was done in two ways: either all is flux (becoming without being–Heraclitus, or all is dukkha, dependently co-arising - Buddhism), or all is permanent (being without becoming – Parmenides, or all is one, beyond all dualities–Shankara's Advaita). Where all is permanent, change is an illusion (maya). Where all is change, permanence is an illusion (no object, no self). Since knowledge of the world involves permanence and change (some change in permanence and some permanence in change), on the assumption that all is one (either change or permanence), knowledge is not possible. The dualism of Plato and Aristotle attempted to address the problem of permanence and change but left significant problems unresolved.

Epistemological skepticism reckons with the limits of experience and reason as they have been used in the modern period (Enlightenment). Experience may come through ordinary sense experience (common sense), or sense experience systematically pursued (science), or through inner experience (intuition). Ordinary experience gives appearance and not reality (Is the ocean blue? Does the sun rise?). Furthermore, through sense experience we cannot know there is an external world or material substance (Berkeley), nor causality or a self as perceiver (Hume). Science does not attempt to show that the external world exists, or that all is matter, or that matter is eternal. Naturalism is the methodological assumption of science and empiricism, held on pragmatic grounds, with a tentativeness which disinvites philosophical criticism. Intuition admits of no corrective process. But neither are the deliverances of intuition self-certifying. Truth (or goodness) is not always connected with beauty, and, what is called

# Foreword

enlightenment experience (nirvana, samadhi) becomes inescapably connected with interpretations which are irreconcilable.

Methodological doubt of ordinary (or extra-ordinary) experience led Descartes to what he took to be the first and indubitable truth of reason (I think, therefore I am), upon which he attempted to erect a superstructure of knowledge (foundationalism). But the *Cogito* became doubted in light of monism (absolute idealism) along with the mind/body and subject/object distinctions. The existence of the self is no more self-evident than the existence of God ("We hold these truths to be self-evident, that all men are created equal"). Furthermore, the traditional proofs for the existence of God (ontological, cosmological, and teleological), taken separately, were found problematic at least, over a period of time. And reason seemed to present us with equally coherent and incommensurable worlds (Leibniz and Spinoza). Kant's synthesis of sense experience and reason left the world beyond appearance (the noumenal world) devoid of cognizable content and open to the speculation which followed. Reason, with its tendency to universalize, was seen as incapable of grasping the particulars of the real world (Nietzsche), or the concrete situation in which all exists (Kierkegaard).

Far from reason being a transcendent standard which gives knowledge of an objective world in which we exist, hermeneutical skepticism holds that reason (as well as science) is itself subject to the situation in which we find ourselves. We are always historically situated and cannot transcend our history. The world we live in is constructed on the basis of our identities and language grounded in our social context. There is no objective world in itself (anti-realism). The canons of rationality differ from one worldview to another. All is interpretation (Nietzsche). We are bound in a hermeneutical circle. Claims to objectivity are attempts to privilege one's own position for advantage over others. It is inevitably repressive of the other, in the name of common standard, defined by one's own meta-narrative. Since all things are understood within the confines of one's meta-narrative, one must recognize incommensurability between worldviews, the reality of alterity, and the ultimacy of difference. This recognition is said to be the virtue of tolerance. Hermeneutical skepticism says our beliefs are inescapably without proof and should be recognized as such. Fideism acquiesces to this.

## II

## Fideism

Fideism applies to all interpretive belief systems which make no attempt to prove its first principles, especially in light of existing challenges to them. It applies to theism as well as to anti-theism, to science as well as to philosophy, to realism as well as to anti-realism, to foundationalism as well as to anti-foundationalism. It occurs whenever reasons given are not sufficient to rationally exclude competing views. While fideism applies to a wide range of views, most discussions have focused on theistic fideism, particularly on Christian fideism. Christians have attempted to give reasons for their beliefs, but, in light of the challenges of skepticism, Christian fideism has responded by maintaining either reason (proof) is not necessary for belief or not sufficient for belief or not called for by scripture.

That reason (proof) is not necessary for belief in God seems obvious since many believe without proof. Many maintain that faith, by definition, is not sight (proof) and many have no idea of the proofs as they have been given historically. Some have argued that reason is not necessary since belief in God is properly basic, like belief in the external world, for which proof seems irrelevant. Properly basic beliefs occur naturally under certain conditions if one's cognitive faculties are properly functioning. Natural belief in God is warranted, without proof, although warrant may be weakened in the presence of objections if they are unanswered (Plantinga). Again, reason is said to be unnecessary for faith since faith is said to precede understanding and that we must believe in order that we might understand. Having first believed, faith then seeks to understand (Augustine). And again, reason is said to be unnecessary since faith is by grace and not a work of human reason (Barth).

Furthermore, reason is said to be insufficient for faith. The proofs do not seem to persuade most people to believe, nor does knowing move someone to act. People are said to know, deep down, the truth of God's existence and yet suppress this truth, and to know what is right and yet do what is wrong. Reason is said to be finite and incapable of discovering or apprehending the mysteries of the faith, which remain paradoxes to the intellect, even after they are made known by revelation. If some are able to come to the truth of first things through dialectic, this is not available to most (Plato's Allegory of the Cave), and is accessible only to few minds which have been trained in metaphysics (Aquinas). Faith is said to be inaccessible to reason. The individual before God, in his unique particularity (Abraham called to sacrifice Isaac), has no guidance possible from reason which deals in universals. Faith is a leap beyond reason (Kierkegaard). Reason is said to be fallen and fallible and its use, apart from revelation, leads man away from God. Reason is said to be conditioned by pre-theoretical commitments so that all proofs are in the end circular, reflecting one's presupposition. And lastly, reason itself is said to be not sufficient for justification but is thought to itself require justification, which can be found only in God, specifically, in the triune God of the Bible (VanTil/Bahnsen).

There are reasons offered for fideism based on appeal to scripture. There are no proofs given in scripture for the existence of God so it is thought that no proof is necessary. This view assumes that everything needed by the believer is expressly given in scripture, and in a form that does not require good and necessary consequences. This view affirms the sole authority of scripture (*sola scriptura*) over against all other authorities, including reason and general revelation, not merely over all other appeals to special revelation and to persons as authorities. It is pointed out that there are warnings raised in scripture against the wisdom of this world, and against vain philosophy (*simpliciter*). There is said to be in scripture an exaltation of proclamation of things foolish in the eyes of the world, and this is understood in a way that excludes reasoning and persuasion. Furthermore, the fullness of blessing is said to be reserved for those faithful in this life who will, in life after death, see God face to face (beatific vision). The highest good therefore does not require and is not accessible to the life of reason.

## III
## The Necessity for Natural Theology

One response to the pressing weight of skepticism and fideism is to make the point that the knowledge of God (and of the world) is not discursive, to be attained by reason and inference. It is more akin to knowledge by experience through acquaintance or encounter. It cannot be expressed in words or communicated to another through words. One must have the experience. This knowledge is non-cognitive (not a matter of true or false), and non-propositional (not to be argued for or against). It is immediate, direct, personal, relational, and mystical, like an embrace.

While it is true enough that thinking is not the same as or a substitute for experience, it is equally the case that experience is not the same as or a substitute for thinking. They are two distinct but inseparable aspects of human knowledge. We don't simply experience but 'experience as.' An embrace has significance in light of assumptions about the other in the embrace, assumptions not derived from the experience itself, assumptions of which we may become more conscious and critical and perhaps change, so that the significance of the embrace may change or deepen over time in one and the same person. No experience is meaningful without interpretation. Any appeal to experience stripped of interpretation becomes meaningless. The shift to non-cognitivism in order to possess knowledge, without engaging with the objections of skepticism and fideism, and without engaging in natural theology, is in vain since experience devoid of meaning is empty. A different strategy is required which can show the inadequacy of both skepticism and fideism, even as non-cognitivism is inadequate.

Skepticism has value. Its value is negative. Its lasting value is that it will not let fideism pass without identifying itself as such. Skepticism is aware of the arbitrariness of fideism when it claims to be objective and exclusive, and finds that arbitrariness self-destructive. But skepticism reaches an over-extended conclusion (that no knowledge is possible) by assuming it has considered all relevant assumptions. There are assumptions which skepticism has not considered. There are alternatives to the assumption of monism (either nothing is eternal or all is eternal). There are alternatives to ontological dualism (both matter and spirit are eternal). Theism, the view that only some (God the creator) is eternal is an alternative to both monism and dualism. There are alternatives to rationalism and to empiricism and to the synthesis of the two, which recognize what is uncritically assumed in both. There are alternatives to science (pure facts without interpretation) and deconstruction (pure interpretation without facts). One can identify and distinguish pure experience/fact (for example, the embrace) from its significance, given by interpretation. If there were no alternatives to the assumptions it has considered, then skepticism would be granted. But if it were granted, and carried out consistently, skepticism would lead to nihilism, the destruction of all meaning by the destruction of all distinctions. Qualified skepticism ("this view is incoherent") is possible; total skepticism ("all views are incoherent") becomes self-referentially absurd.

Fideism, too, has value, and its value is positive. It recognizes the impossibility of nihilism to which skepticism leads, and the inadequacy of pragmatism to overcome self-conscious nihilism. Positions of fideism purport to offer its adherents a meaningful vision of the world. A more self-conscious fideism maintains its right to exist by an exclusivist claim to truth and meaning. But fideism wishes to make some distinction between faith and understanding. In the motto "faith seeking understanding" it is assumed that one can believe more than one understands. If it were possible to believe more than one understands then one could believe what one did not understand. To open a gap between believing $p$ to be true and understanding $p$ is to affirm $p$ while emptying $p$ of meaning. I believe $p$ as far as I understand $p$. There is more to understand of $p$, and I seek to understand more of $p$ but I do not and cannot believe more than I understand. If "faith seeking understanding" means "understanding seeking more understanding" there is nothing controversial here. By faith I believe $p$ to be true; by reason I understand the meaning of $p$. As truth is inseparable from meaning so faith is inseparable from reason. It is not the case that faith is static and understanding grows in "faith seeking understanding." Faith grows as understanding grows; faith is tested as understanding is tested.

Faith, in the theistic sense, is directed to what is invisible. Faith is contrasted with sight, which is directed to the visible, but it is not contrasted with understanding which is directed to what is invisible. Faith in Christian theism is being sure of what is hoped for and certain of what is not seen (Hebrews 11). Since faith is inseparable from understanding, the certainty of faith is the certainty of understanding. The certainty of understanding in faith is not different from the certainty of understanding a proof for what is unseen. Fideism, therefore, insofar as it separates faith and understanding, empties faith of meaning and nullifies its purpose, which is to offer its adherents a meaningful vision of the world. But insofar as it does not separate faith and understanding, it has the certainty of proof in its understanding. So true faith, contrary to fideism, is inseparable from reason, understanding, certainty, and proof. Faith, without reason and proof, that is, fideism, is empty of meaning. Fideism fails in the same way that skepticism fails. Both fail to preserve meaning. Both failures make natural theology necessary.

There is a third set of reasons why natural theology is necessary. Historic Christianity is structured on the theme of Creation, Fall, and

Redemption. The implications of each of these, when understood, requires NT. Historic Christianity assumes the reality of sin. Since sin is a reality in Christianity, Christianity must give some account of sin. Unbelief is regarded as root sin. Unbelief is inexcusable because there is a clear general revelation of the existence and nature of God in the creation. "Since the creation of the world God's invisible qualities – his eternal power and divine nature – have been clearly seen, being understood from what is made, so that men are without excuse (Romans 1:20)." Men are without excuse for unbelief of what is clear. If there is no clarity of general revelation for which one is held accountable there can be no sin. But if there is clarity of general revelation then presumably one should be able to see what is clear. And since it is clear one should be able to show what is clear, especially over against objections which would deny clarity. To see what is clear is to see why the denial of clarity fails. Christian theists, believing in the reality of sin, should be able to show what is clear. To do so would be to do natural theology.

Historic Christianity not only affirms the reality of sin but it affirms divine judgment on sin. The wages of sin is death (Romans 6). This death is present in unbelief in this life and in the life to come. This death is spiritual and is inherent in unbelief. It is the meaninglessness that is inherent in the failure to see what is clear at the most basic level of all of one's understanding. This death is also said to be everlasting. Everlasting death is maximal consequence. Maximal consequence requires maximal inexcusability, which in turn requires maximal clarity. The contradiction of what is maximally clear is not logically possible. Maximal clarity can be avoided only by ceasing to think, that is, to give up or to deny reason itself. Natural theology in Christian theism must show maximal clarity.

Historic Christianity affirms redemption. Christ is the Lamb of God who takes away the sin of the world. If sense is to be made of the death of Christ by which sin and death are removed, then clarity and inexcusability must be shown by natural theology.

Historic Christianity has been exclusivist, believing that redemption is through Christ alone. It also believes that Christ's redemption is for all peoples. If people are called away from competing worldviews to the Christian worldview, reasons for the truth of its exclusive claims which do not beg the question must be given. This requires natural theology.

Historic Christianity holds up the highest good and the goal of life as the knowledge of God. Creation and history reveal God. Through an age-long and agonizing spiritual war good will overcome evil. The earth shall be full of the knowledge of God as the waters cover the sea. If God's justice and mercy are to be understood, the inexcusability of unbelief must be understood. If we do not understand clarity then we cannot understand inexcusability. But if we understand clarity then we can show clarity. This is the work of natural theology.

## IV
## What is Reason?

Some clarification in the understanding of reason is necessary in order to show more specifically how knowledge is possible. There are different senses of reason that must be kept clearly in mind whenever the term 'reason' and its derivatives are used. There is first, reason in itself, to be distinguished from reason in its use and reason in us. There are different uses of reason and different aspects of reason in us.

Reason in itself is the laws of thought. These laws are most basically the law of identity ($a$ is $a$), the law of non-contradiction (not both $a$ and *non-a* in the same respect and the same time), and the law of excluded middle (either $a$ or *non-a*). These, minimally, have been commonly accepted in the history of philosophy as the laws of reason and the laws of thought. 'Finite' and 'fallen' may apply to human users of these laws but not to the laws themselves. They may apply to the failure to use reason critically rather than a failure of reason itself. When any of these laws are broken reason is not being used and thinking ceases.

Reason is used to form concepts, judgments, and arguments which are the forms of all thought. Reason is used critically as a test of meaning. Meaning is more basic than truth. We must know what a statement means before we can know if it is true. When a law of thought is violated there is no meaning. Reason is used to interpret experience in light of one's basic beliefs. And reason is used constructively to construct a coherent world and life view. The constructive use of reason is not the same as the critical use. Reason should be used critically first to test one's basic beliefs for meaning, before constructing a worldview upon them. Likewise, the interpretive use must be distinguished from the critical use. Much confusion in hermeneutical skepticism can be avoided by observing some of these distinctions.

Reason in itself is natural, not conventional. It is universal, the same in all persons. It is a common ground between all worldviews. It is the source of coherence in constructing a worldview and in the test for meaning of its basic beliefs. It is the common ground by which thoughts (concepts, judgments, and arguments) are formed and that by which experience is interpreted in light of basic beliefs. Reason in itself as common ground is not historically situated; it is universal. This prevents incommensurability between worldviews, even when basic beliefs in different worldviews are contradictory.

Reason is ontological. It applies to being as well as to thought. There are no square-circles, no uncaused events, no being from non-being. God is not both eternal and not eternal in the same respect and at the same time. If reason did not apply to being then statements could be true and not true in the same respect and at the same time. If *a* could be *non-a*, then being could not be distinguished from non-being. All distinctions would lose meaning, and all meaning would be lost.

Reason is transcendental. It is authoritative. It is self-attesting, the highest authority. It cannot be questioned because it makes questioning possible. A statement which violates a law of reason is not meaningful and cannot be true, regardless of its source.

Reason is also fundamental. It is fundamental to other aspects of human personality. Thought supplies the belief concerning the good as the object of desire. And thought and desire move a person to act. It is knowing the truth that sets a person free.

Thinking is presuppositional. This follows from the nature of reason in itself, reason in its use and reason in us. We think of what is less basic in light of what is more basic. We think of truth in light of meaning; we think of experience in light of basic belief; we think of conclusion in light of premises; we think of the temporal in light of the eternal, and the finite in light of the infinite. We must know what a statement means before we can know if it is true. If it violates a law of reason it is not meaningful because reason, as the laws of thought, is transcendental – it is the test for meaning, and thus of what can and cannot be true. If a statement is meaningless it cannot be true because reason is ontological. If there is agreement on what is more basic (that reason is the laws of thought, universal, ontological, and transcendental) there can be agreement on what is less basic. If there is doubt that reason is ontological, disagreement is not even possible because skepticism here lapses into nihilism and the loss of meaning.

Since thinking is presuppositional, and reason, as the test for meaning, is most basic, this position can be described as rational presuppositionalism. It is a position distinct from empiricism, rationalism, and fideistic presuppositionalism.

## V

The first application of Rational Presuppositionalism: show there must be something eternal. The first act of reason is in forming concepts, and the most basic concept is about existence. Since existence is either temporal (with beginning) or eternal (without beginning), and since eternal is more basic than temporal, our most basic concept is about eternal existence. The possible judgments concerning what is eternal are four: all is eternal; none is eternal; some is eternal; and some is not eternal. Can we know if there is something eternal? The following is offered as proof that something must be eternal:

1. Contradictory statements cannot both be truth and both be false.
2. The contradiction of 'some is eternal' is 'none is eternal.'
3. If nothing is eternal then:
    a. All is temporal.
    b. All had a beginning.
    c. All came into being.
    d. If all came into being then being came into existence from non-being.
    e. Being from non-being is not possible.
    f. Therefore the original 'none is eternal' is not possible.
    g. Therefore its contradictory 'some is eternal' must be true.

Being comes from being alone. Non-being is the absence of being and of the power of being to cause to be. If being could come from non-being then there would be no distinction between being and non-being ('$a$' could be '$non\text{-}a$'). Skepticism and nihilism are the result.

It is clear through reason therefore that something must be eternal. To doubt this one must give up reason. To give up reason is to give up meaning. 'There must be something eternal' is maximally clear. The opposite is not possible. To doubt what is maximally clear one must give up reason. To give up reason is to deny one's nature as a rational being and so to bring upon oneself spiritual death, which is meaninglessness.

## VI

## The Program of Natural Theology

The goal of NT is to show what is clear about God and man and good and evil from general revelation. It is to respond to all objections raised against the knowledge of God, proceeding from what is most basic in general revelation to what is equally basic in special revelation. It must show all that is clear from general revelation which is necessary for inexcusability, as well as respond to philosophical objections to the doctrines of special revelation. What follows is an outline of the objectives by which this goal is to be achieved. The objectives state what must be done and indicate only in the most general way how this may be done.

1. Show that there must be something eternal. Since eternal is our most basic concept and since God is eternal, it must be shown that there must be something eternal. This first step is necessary but not sufficient to prove the existence of God. This proof is a modification of the ontological argument: what cannot be logically conceived cannot exist.
2. Show that only some is eternal. Since God is creator of all things, only some (God) is eternal. All else is temporal. This step uses the cosmological argument in a variety of ways.
3. The material world is not eternal (vs. material monism). It is not self-maintaining in general (entropy), in its parts (sun and stars) and as a whole (the big bang oscillating universe or the inflationary universe).
4. The material world exists (vs. ordinary idealism – Berkeley). The cause of what I see is not my mind or another mind but outside all minds.
5. The soul exists - the mind is not the brain (vs. material monism). A neural impulse is not a mental image, nor does the mental image perceive itself.
6. The soul is not eternal (vs. ordinary dualism – Plato, and qualified non-dualism – Ramanuja). The soul goes through unique events in time (growth in knowledge, enlightenment, etc.).
7. The soul exists (vs. absolute idealism, Advaita – Shankara). The soul is neither unreal, that is, an illusion/maya, nor real/eternal).
8. Respond to the problem of evil. If God is all good and all powerful why is there evil? The teleological argument is used to respond to the problem of natural evil and moral evil.

Foreword                          xvii

    a. Natural evil (toil, strife, old age, sickness and death) is not necessary. Original creation was very good, without natural evil (vs. origin by evolution, natural or theistic).
    b. Natural evil is due to moral evil. It is imposed, not as punishment, but as a call back from moral evil. Suffering is a call to stop and think.
    c. Moral evil is permitted for a purpose; it is made to serve the good through deepening of the divine revelation.
    d. There is an ironic solution to the problem of evil, requiring understanding the nature of evil in light of the clarity of general revelation.

9. Show the moral law from general revelation. If there is not a moral law which is clear from general revelation then human responsibility and moral evil are not possible. This moral law must be clear, comprehensive, and critical.
    a. The moral law is clear because it is grounded in the fundamental features of human nature. It is grounded in the reality of choice, in the nature of thinking, in the natural unity of our being, in the work required to bring into being and sustain in being, in being born ignorant, in being born human, in being of a sexual union, in valuing and producing what is of value, in being born equal, in being born changeable.
    b. The moral law is comprehensive in that it applies to all choices and all aspects of human nature which come to expression in choice.
    c. The moral law is critical. The consequence of observing the moral law is life, which is, obtaining the good; the consequence of not observing the law is spiritual death, both individual and corporate.

10. From deism to theism.
    a. Deism maintains that God creates but does not act in history.
    b. Theism (Judaism, Christianity, and Islam) maintains that God creates and acts providentially in history including, specifically, in giving scriptures.
    c. God acts in history in imposing natural evil. Natural evil is not in the original creation and not inherent in moral evil.

d. Natural evil as a call back from moral evil requires redemptive revelation to show how God can be both just and merciful.
   e. Special revelation must be consistent with general revelation and must show how God is both just and merciful.
   f. Biblical revelation only is consistent with general revelation and shows how God is both just and merciful.
11. The root of conflict among theists.
   a. Judaism, Christianity, and Islam profess to hold to some basic scriptures in common. Since scripture is redemptive revelation, the conflict between them is rooted in their understanding of the divine nature regarding how God is both just and merciful in redemption.
   b. Judaism and Christianity affirm that God is both just and merciful by nature and that mercy must satisfy divine justice by atonement. Islam affirms that God has no nature by which he is bound; mercy can set aside divine justice – there is no need for atonement
   c. Biblical Judaism affirms the justice and mercy of God in vicarious atonement through the death of another as seen in the Temple sacrifice on the Day of Atonement. Post-Biblical Judaism affirms that atonement is in and by oneself.
   d. Christianity affirms the justice and mercy of God in vicarious atonement through human representation (Christ in the place of Adam). The lamb symbolically represented Christ, in whose death the reality of atonement is accomplished
12. Rational challenges to doctrines of Christianity. Non-theists and non-Christian theists have objected to ecumenical doctrines in Christianity. If scripture is divine revelation it must be shown that these doctrines, while not originating from human reasoning, are in accordance with reason and are consistent with all that can be expected from both general and special revelation.
   a. The doctrine of the Trinity requires an understanding of what is meant in saying "God is one."
   b. The doctrine of the Incarnation requires an understanding of unity and diversity of two natures in one person.
   c. The doctrine of the Fall requires an understanding of the nature of moral evil (sin) and of representation.

13. Philosophical questions in the continuing divisions within Christianity. Redemptive revelation in scripture assumes the reality of sin in the failure to understand clear general revelation. Understanding scripture assumes the understanding of general revelation. Continuing divisions within Christianity reveal lack in understanding what is clear in general revelation. The perspicuity of scripture rests on the clarity of general revelation.
    a. There is continuing division concerning the sufficiency of vicarious atonement (grace vs. works).
    b. There is continuing division concerning divine sovereignty in predestination and human freedom and responsibility.
    c. There is continuing division concerning hermeneutics: what is literal and what is contextual interpretation, and what is the order within contextual layers.
    d. There is continuing division concerning the good: is the knowledge of God gained through a direct vision of God in heaven or is it the knowledge of God gained through the work of dominion on earth through history?

## Conclusion

Natural theology, I believe, is not only possible. It is necessary. The external and internal challenges to Christian theism have accumulated through the Enlightenment period, although they have roots going back into ancient history. The need for natural theology today is more urgent, if not acute, as ancient worldviews come face to face. All human beings need meaning, and neither skepticism nor fideism can provide that meaning for human beings as they become more epistemologically self-conscious and consistent. A deeper understanding of reason, leading to a deeper, clearer and more consistent understanding of good and evil, can lead us out of our present impasse, to a unity and fullness we had not thought was possible. In the present post-Christian, Post-Modern milieu, the necessity for natural theology has become pressing. Mr. Anderson's analysis of recent contributors to this dialogue is therefore both valuable and timely.

Surrendra Gangadean
May, 2005
Phoenix, Az

## Acknowledgments:

I would like to thank Professors Moses Moore, Michael White, and Eugene Clay for their help on this project. I am indebted to my parents, John and Leanna Anderson, to Keith Makedonsky, and to Brandon Crowe, for their careful reading and suggestions. I owe special thanks to Surrendra Gangadean for his help over the years. And most importantly, I wish to thank my wife, Sherry, who read and listened to the many versions of this work, and without whose help it would not have been finished.


Owen Anderson
Phoenix, Az
May, 2005

## Introduction:

The Apostle Peter encourages his audience to "always be ready to give a defense to everyone who asks you a reason for the hope that is in you" (1 Peter 3:15, NKJV). Such a defense is the goal of apologetics. Throughout the history of Christianity apologetics has been assigned different functions and importance. While these differences depend on various factors, central to these is the epistemological framework of the particular apologist. In order to defend the faith the apologist must know what a defense is, and the content of the faith being defended. In keeping with this admonition Benjamin B. Warfield (1851-1921) gave an apologetical system that centered its epistemology on the concept of "right reason." As the last of the Old School Princeton Theologians, one implication of Warfield's apologetical system is that God's existence can be known by reason through general revelation. This work will examine Warfield and his legacy specifically with respect to his claim that reason can be used to know God, and how this consequently gives to apologetics the task of showing the inexcusability of unbelief.

*Benjamin B. Warfield: Right Reason and Apologetics* aims to contribute to the study of Warfield an examination of the role and function of inexcusability and clarity in Warfield's approach to apologetics, and more specifically to knowing God. Christianity claims that humanity is inexcusable in its ignorance of God's nature and power (Romans chapter 1). The Apostle Paul begins his systematic statement of Christian doctrine (the book of Romans) by saying "For since the creation of the world His invisible attributes are clearly seen, being understood by the things that are made, even His eternal power and Godhead, so that they are without excuse" (Rom 1:20, NKJV). What can be known of God is revealed to all in a clear general revelation. "The heavens declare the glory of God; And the firmament shows His handiwork" (Psalm 19:1, NKJV). This means that all people at all times can know God. Accordingly, it is the rejection of the knowledge of God found in creation that leaves humanity inexcusable, and in need of redemption. Warfield echoes this when he says:

> This primary idea of God, in which is summed up what is known as theism, is the product of that general revelation which God makes of Himself to all men, on the plan of nature. The truths involved in it are continually reiterated, enriched, and deepened in the Scriptures; but they are not so much revealed by them as presupposed at the foundation of the special revelation with which the Scriptures busy themselves.[1]

One of the distinctive claims of Christianity is that humans need redemption and that this redemption comes through Christ. This claim carries with it some important assumptions. First, the need for redemption assumes guilt. That a person needs to be redeemed first assumes that the person is guilty of something. The Apostle Paul claims that humans are guilty in their failure to know God. Second, if a person is guilty in their failure to know God this assumes that the person could have known God. This means that there must be a general revelation of God to all humans in order for unbelief to be inexcusable. And third, this general revelation of God must be readily knowable, or clear, in order for there to be inexcusability, guilt, and the need for redemption. God's existence must be knowable through the use of reason to all humans. If it is not, then unbelief has an excuse, and the claim that humans need redemption from guilt is unfounded. This gives a very clear project for apologetics: show that God's existence is knowable by reason through a clear general revelation to all humans so that unbelief is without an excuse. Without this foundation the rest of the Christian message about redemption and Christ will not make sense. It will be on this basis that Warfield, Kuyper, and VanTil are analyzed: to what extent does their epistemology and apologetical method support the clarity of general revelation as a necessary presupposition to the Christian message of redemption?

Warfield's emphasis on "right reason" is closely connected to the need for clarity and inexcusability, and leads therefore to his stress on the need for apologetics. At the same time, there are aspects of his approach that might lead to what is called "evidentialism." Evidentialism uses evidences to inductively arrive at the truth of Christianity, and consequently only establishes the probability of Christianity. The problem with this approach is that it does not establish the inexcusability of unbelief and therefore does not give a foundation for the need for redemption. It is helpful to understand Warfield in the context of Princeton Theological Seminary and Scottish Common Sense Philosophy which was the epistemology of choice at Princeton. Princeton Theological Seminary's stated purpose was to educate youth for the ministry with an emphasis on understanding and defending the Reformed faith. In his essay on Warfield, W. Andrew Hoffecker notes that A. Alexander[2] passed his mantle to Charles Hodge, giving with it the guarding of this original purpose.[3] The passing of A. Alexander's mantle to Charles Hodge[4] and then A.A. Hodge[5] is symbolic of the continuity of thought and agenda between these theologians. Princeton was proud that it had not changed in the face of continued intellectual attacks from sources such as Arminianism, Deism, and Unitarianism over the course of the 19th century. This tradition continued more or less consistently until 1929 when the faculty split and some left to start Westminster Theological Seminary to preserve what they believed to be the Princeton tradition.

The epistemology adopted by Princeton Theological lent itself to a defense of the faith in line with clarity and inexcusability. Thomas Reid[6] developed the Scottish Common Sense Philosophy in the latter part of the eighteenth century. In it he argued, "perception involves both sensation and certain intuitively known general truths or principles that together yield knowledge of external objects."[7] Reid argued this directly against the skepticism of David Hume, and Reid's system stands in contrast to Immanuel Kant's attempt at avoiding this same skepticism.[8] "I observed that Mr. Hume's argument not only has no strength to support his conclusion, but that it leads to the contrary conclusion."[9] Reid argued that these intuitively known truths are knowable by all normal humans. The Princeton Theologians took this idea and applied it to apologetics in order to support the claim that there is a clear general revelation. This Common Sense Philosophy provided Princeton an expression of epistemology that had important similarities with Augustine and Calvin.[10] The views of general revelation that Princeton rejected were those that said either general revelation is not clear and does not reveal God, or that general revelation is faint, revealing a little but not much. In contrast Princetonians like Charles Hodge argued that the revelation of God's nature is clear enough to hold men without excuse. "Epistemologically, for liberalism (via Kant), metaphysics was out; for Warfield and Princeton (via the Bible, they would say), metaphysics was still in. There were now two mutually exclusive theological viewpoints; and Princeton was the most vigorous opponent of the new approach. Princeton University president James McCosh decried the new point of view, saying 'There is a need of a rebellion against Kant's despotic authority'."[11]

Princeton's view of the relationship between general and special revelation is also important. The Princetonians argued against those who said that general revelation reveals the world while special revelation reveals God and redemption, or that God can be known through special revelation only. In contrast to such positions Warfield argued that one must first see that God exists in order to have the message of special revelation authenticated.

The Common Sense Philosophy does have some ambiguities however, especially connected to what the "intuitions" known by all are. Reliance on these "intuitions" often leads to fideism, and fideism undermines the needs for redemption by denying that there is a clear, general revelation. Because the Princetonians argued that a knowledge of God is one of these, this will have bearing on their understanding of how God is known. One common position says that God is known through an innate knowledge that all humans have and suppress. This leads to a situation where people both know and do not know at the same time, and a vague definition of the nature of God and what is known about God. Or perhaps the intuition is a feeling, like the sense of love. However the Apostle Paul states that much more can be known of God through general revelation than a mere sense of love (for example God's eternal power and divine nature). Another option is that God's existence can be shown to be highly likely or probable, however probability does not arrive at inexcusability. This is different than the existence of God being clear (e.g. Warfield's view of right reason) and thus leaving men without excuse, which is a fourth option. The relationship between the Princeton Theologians and Scottish Common Sense Philosophy helps to clarify their position while at the same time creating ambiguities central to the debate between B.B. Warfield and Abraham Kuyper.

While Warfield's emphasis is on right reason, Kuyper's emphasis is on the relation of beliefs to worldviews (*Weltanschauung*). It is on this point that the two thinkers differ. Kuyper emphasizes that a person's beliefs are a part of an entire worldview. Hence there is the worldview of believers, and the worldview of unbelievers. These two are not reconcilable, and they are working on different projects. What the believers call science, the unbelievers will deny as science, and vice versa. This view gives little importance to apologetics since while a believer may offer a sound argument to an unbeliever, the unbeliever will not recognize it as such. Warfield affirms many aspects of Kuyper's system, and certainly agrees that there are competing worldviews. However he sees the unbeliever's worldview as inherently self-contradictory. The only way that the unbeliever can come to know anything is by being inconsistent and failing to use reason at some point. This inconsistency can be shown to the unbeliever, and herein is part of the job of apologetics.

The legacy of Warfield is not necessarily to be found at Princeton. In 1929 Princeton Theological split and a number of the faculty members left to form Westminster Theological. One of those that left Princeton to help found Westminster was Cornelius VanTil[12] (1895-1987). Born in Holland, and having studied at Princeton, VanTil had a deep understanding of both Kuyper and Warfield. His Presuppositionalism is an attempt to find and emphasize the best in both, while avoiding what he saw as mistakes on each side. Specifically, while VanTil agreed with Kuyper that there are two worldviews existing in mutually exclusive spheres, and that only one is doing science, he agreed with Warfield that it is the Christian presuppositions that allow for knowledge. However, it is not the "right reason" that Warfield outlines, but the Bible itself that provides the foundation for knowledge. To set the Bible up to be scrutinized by a non-Biblical standard is to put God in the defendant's seat and in so doing judge God by a false standard. VanTil argued that God cannot be judged and that His revelation speaks for itself and provides the only possible basis for knowledge. As above, the issue of inexcusability will be the emphasis in looking at Warfield's successors at Westminster. If Scripture is the only standard for knowledge, how are unbelievers inexcusable in their unbelief Warfield's appeal to right reason will provide the answer to this in that reason is not an arbitrary standard used to judge God, nor is it only available to those with access to the Bible.

In conclusion, the necessity for rationality, clarity, and inexcusability will be explored. If Warfield's apologetical method can help solve problems facing contemporary Christian apologetics, these assumptions of the Christian worldview must be better understood. The history and figures looked at in this account demonstrate how the notion of inexcusability in Christian apologetics has been developed in the Christian tradition up to the present. Concerning the role of apologetics Warfield argued: "the part that Apologetics has to play in the Christianizing of the world is rather a primary part, and it is a conquering part."[13] Such a role cannot possibly be fulfilled if the content of the message cannot be known by reason. In contrast to the anti-rationalism of Kierkegaard and Neo-Orthodoxy, the Princetonians, and later the Presuppositionalists, argued for the ultimate rationality of Christianity and the inherent inconsistency of all other worldviews. Christianity claims to have a message of redemption for all people. This assumes that all people need redemption. Warfield's apologetical method is much more consistent with the assumptions behind the Christian message of redemption than are other methods. The following will explore his method, and draw out some implications about reason and general revelation.

Notes

1. Benjamin Breckinridge Warfield, *Studies in Theology*, Grand Rapids: Baker Book House, 2000. 109.
2. Archibald Alexander (1772-1851) was a founding professor of Princeton Theological Seminary in 1812. He was influenced by the Rev. William Graham, a president of Princeton College. Before teaching at Princeton he served as the president of Hampden-Sydney College.
3. W. Andrew Hoffecker, "Benjamin B. Warfield," in *Reformed Theology in America*, ed. Wells, David (Grand Rapids: Baker Books, 1997), 65.
4. Charles Hodge (1797-1878) taught at Princeton from 1822 until 1878, with an exception of two years spent studying in Germany. His *Systematic Theology* replaced Turretin's *Institutio Theologiae Elencticae* at Princeton as the text for theology.
5. A.A. Hodge (1823-1886), son of Charles Hodge, and named after A. Alexander, taught at Princeton for ten years.
6. Thomas Reid (1710-1796) was a Scottish philosopher. He attended Marischal College in Aberdeen, and later taught at King's College in Aberdeen. He is known for his defense of common sense against David Hume's skepticism.
7. Robert Audi, ed., *The Cambridge Dictionary of Philosophy* (Cambridge: Cambridge University Press, 1999), 822.
8. Kant argued that Reid failed to understand Hume's argument ("Prolegomena to Any Future Metaphysics" in *Modern Philosophy*, ed. by Forrest E. Baird and Walter Kaufmann (New Jersey: Prentice Hall, 1997), 532-602. 534).
9. Thomas Reid, "Essays on the Intellectual Powers of Man," in *Modern Philosophy*, ed. Forrest E. Baird and Walter Kaufmann (New Jersey: Prentice Hall, 1997), 484.
10. "The modern factors of historicism, sociology, and scientific method and outlook undercut the traditional views of the Bible, the supernatural, and any form of objective truth from beyond. Princeton Seminary and Warfield stood against these reinterpretations of reality, maintaining that there was a truth revealed to human beings from God" (James S McClanahan, "Benjamin B Warfield : Historian of Doctrine in Defense of Orthodoxy 1881-1921," *Affirmation* 6 (Fall 1993): 89-111. 93.).
11. James S. McClanahan, "Benjamin B Warfield : Historian of Doctrine in Defense of Orthodoxy 1881-1921." *Affirmation* 6 (Fall 1993): 89-111. 93.
12. Cornelius VanTil was born in Grootegast, Holland. At age ten he left from Rotterdam for the U.S. and settled with his family at Highland, Indiana. In 1914 he began attending Calvin Preparatory School and College. In 1921 he enrolled at Calvin Theological Seminary. He transferred in 1922 to Princeton, where he studied both at the seminary and the university. In 1927 he earned a Ph.D in philosophy, and lectured at the seminary from 1928-29. In 1929 VanTil became one of the founding professors at Westminster Theological Seminary where he taught for more than 40 years. He is known for his "presuppositional" approach to apologetics.
13. Warfield, "Introduction," in *Apologetics*, 26.

# Chapter 1:
# Princeton Theological Seminary and Common Sense Philosophy

Old School Princeton Theological Seminary stood out in its time for its dedication to the rational justification of the Reformed Presbyterian faith. One distinguishing mark of Princeton was its reliance on Reformed Confessions, particularly the Westminster Confession of Faith.[1] The first article of this confession begins by saying: "The light of nature, and the works of creation and providence do so far manifest the goodness, wisdom, and power of God as to leave men unexcusable." In this section of the Confession is affirmed all that was derived above from Romans 1:20. God's nature is clearly seen by the light of nature (reason), in creation, and in providence. It is the failure to see the nature of God in these that leaves humanity inexcusable and in need of redemption. The knowledge of how this redemption is accomplished is found only in the Scriptures. However, reason, creation, and providence still clearly reveal God to all and continue to hold humans accountable for knowing their Creator. In this chapter it will be argued that Princeton Theological attempted to formulate an epistemology (influenced by Scottish Common Sense Philosophy) that upheld clarity and the ability to know God, and therefore also maintained, at least by implication, inexcusability with respect to unbelief.

Princeton Theological Seminary began in 1812, although Archibald Alexander, one of its first professors, proposed the idea of a new Presbyterian Seminary in 1808.[2] Alexander said at the General Assembly of 1808 that "In my opinion we shall not have a regular and sufficient supply of well qualified ministers of the gospel, until every presbytery, or at least every synod, shall have under its direction a seminary established for the single purpose of educating youth for the ministry, in which the course of education from its commencement shall be directed to this object."³ Plans began to be set in motion for what would be Princeton Theological Seminary. The purpose statement was initially drafted by Ashbel Green in 1810, and was altered imperceptibly by the General Assembly of the Presbyterian Church in 1811. "This seminal document contained the philosophy of theological education which Alexander and his successors adhered to closely, a philosophy impregnated with Scottish Realism."⁴ The plan of the Seminary included an article titled "Of Study and Attainments," giving the objectives to be expected of students by the end of their third year. By this time the student was to "have laid the foundation for becoming a sound biblical critic; . . . a defender of the Christian faith; . . . an able and sound divine and casuist, . . . a useful preacher and a faithful pastor."⁵ Marion Taylor, in the book *The Old Testament in the Old Princeton School (1812-1929)*, states that the intention of the Biblical studies was not heuristic, but instead was a continuation of the philosophical presuppositions of the school focused mainly on apologetic functions. "Central to the seminary's mission statement was the training for gospel ministry of men 'to propagate and defend . . . that system of religious belief and practice which is set forth in the Confession of Faith, Catechisms, and Plan of Government and Discipline of the Presbyterian Church; . . . [and] to provide for the Church, men who shall be able to defend her faith against infidels, and her doctrines against heretics'."⁶ Thus the central focus/role of apologetics was a direct implication of the philosophical presuppositions, particularly Scottish Realism and its claim that knowledge is possible. "The defensive or apologetic orientation towards the study of the Scriptures which grew out of the seminary's mandate became one of the hallmarks of the Old Princeton approach."⁷

Notice that Taylor sees Scottish Realism as a distinguishing mark of the Seminary. "Together with the apologetic bent of the proposed curriculum, this feature was consistent with the 'external' approach to knowledge characteristic of Scottish Realism."⁸ Mark Noll, in his "The Princeton Theology" that appears in *Reformed Theology in America*, sees this philosophical influence as one of four points that stand out as distinctive of the Seminary. The other three distinctive points are the Princetonian's reliance on Reformed Confessions, their view of Scripture, and their view of the work of the Holy Spirit. Scottish Realism affirms the ability of humanity to know, and gives standards for what does and does not count as knowledge.

In his inaugural address of 1812, A. Alexander affirmed the possibility of knowledge and outlined a method to attain the truth. First a truth seeker had to ascertain that the Scriptures do in fact contain truths from God; secondly, he also had to understand what these truths are. To accomplish the first, the student must study the canon of the Old and New Testaments, including their consistency, authenticity, and inspiration. An evidentialist approach was taken to establish the authenticity and inspiriation of the scriptures, by considering miracles, prophecy, and the social and personal benefits of the gospel. And finally, Alexander faulted the deists and others for not holding scritpure as the sufficient and authoritative rule of faith.[9] Here is a clear statement of the epistemology of Princeton. There is a particular emphasis on evidences and proof. Warfield echoed this when he said that before a person can trust the Scriptures as authoritative it must first be proven that they are God's Word, and that there is a God who can be known.[10] Thus there is some standard for knowing that is not derived from Scripture but is used to know more basic truths such as "what counts as Scripture?" It is this that will be examined here in order to see if Princeton's form of "rationality" produces the clarity needed for inexcusability.

It follows from the importance of Alexander's influence as a founding professor at Princeton that his instructors had an indirect influence also worthy of note. Of particular importance to Alexander was William Graham (1746-1799), Alexander's instructor at Princeton College, who in turn had been instructed by John Witherspoon (1723-1794) in Scottish philosophy. Witherspoon brought this teaching with him to America from Scotland where he had been influenced by such thinkers as Francis Hutcheson (1694-1746) and Thomas Reid (1710-1796). Mark Noll sees this philosophy as attempting to "rescue the English 'moderate' Enlightenment of Isaac Newton and John Locke from the skepticism of David Hume and the idealism of George Berkeley."[11] Alexander expressed this position as including an affirmation of the "common sense" of humankind and its ability to verify the physical senses and intuitive consciousness/moral sense. The tradition at Princeton Theological Seminary that started with Alexander passed next to Charles Hodge who was also heavily influenced by this Scottish philosophy. "Hodge's debt to the Scottish Philosophy appears most clearly in the opening pages of his *Systematic Theology* where, in oft-quoted lines, he likened the construction of dogmatic systems to scientific exploration."[12] Charles Hodge's son, A.A. Hodge, similarly accepted this philosophy. Warfield was taught this system by James McCosh who came to Princeton from Scotland in 1868, the year that Warfield began his undergraduate studies.

Mark Noll points out that the Common Sense Philosophy stands in an important relation both to the "moderate" English Enlightenment, and to David Hume's skepticism. George Marsden makes a similar connection, although he breaks the Enlightenment into four parts. The first "is the early Moderate Enlightenment associated with Newton and Locke - the ideals of order, balance, and religious compromise. Second is the Skeptical Enlightenment, represented best by Voltaire and Hume. Third is the Revolutionary Enlightenment - the search for a new heaven on earth - that grew out of the thought of Rousseau. And fourth is the Didactic Enlightenment, stemming from Scottish Common Sense thought, which opposed skepticism and revolution but rescued the essentials of the earlier eighteenth-century commitments to science, rationality, order, and the Christian tradition."[13] Marsden sees only the first and the fourth as having lasting influence in the United States. Important for this book is the assumption behind the first phase of the Enlightenment that humanity can know, and the refutation of Humean skepticism in the fourth phase by Thomas Reid (1710-1796).

Thomas Reid was educated at Marischal College in Aberdeen. There, he studied with Thomas Blackwell and George Turnbull. Turnbull affected Reid greatly with his argument that knowledge of the facts of sense and introspection may not be overturned by reasoning.[14] Reid himself thought that one of his major contributions was a refutation of David Hume's theory of impressions and ideas. Marsden sees this as following from Reid's firm commitment to induction and empiricism.[15] "Reid himself was a great admirer of [Francis] Bacon, the early seventeenth-century philosopher of science. The influence of "'Lord Bacon' on Reid, Dugald Stewart observed approvingly, 'may be traced on almost every page'."[16] Reid claimed that Bacon had taught Newton to despise hypotheses as fictions, and Newton in turn argued that the correct method of philosophy is the induction of real facts from observation and experiment. This sort of induction rests largely on the assumption that there are some certainties that serve as a foundation to all knowledge. "Typically these foundational certitudes include our states of consciousness (such as, I am awake), self-evidently necessary truths (such as 1+2 equals 3), and perhaps those things evident to the senses (I am sure I see a tree over there)."[17] Hume pointed out that these could not be supported by the empirical method advocated by John Locke. Hume argued that men have no way of knowing if the information from their senses corresponds to some object outside of their mind. Thus Hume used reason to cast doubt on empirical evidence and consequently produce skepticism. Reid said that Hume "tells us that 'this universal and primary opinion of all men [direct awareness of external objects] is soon destroyed by the slightest philosophy, which teaches us that nothing can ever be present to the mind but an image or perception."[18]

Reid responded to Hume's skeptical method, and in so doing made plain his intention to establish a foundation for knowledge. Reid argued that all reasoning is based on a foundation, and that the first principles that make up this foundation yield some conclusions that are certain. For example, Reid said, "it is therefore acknowledged by this philosopher to be a natural instinct or prepossession, a universal and primary opinion of all men, a primary instinct of nature, that the objects which we immediately perceive by our senses are not images in our minds, but external objects, and that their existence is independent of us and our perception."[19] Here can be seen something of the concern for rationality and certainty. Reid claimed that these first principles, or basic beliefs, are held as such because they are found in everyone, and those devoid of such beliefs would everywhere be considered a lunatic. He also claimed that they are the foundation of all reasoning. Reid objected to Hume's questioning of principles that Reid believed were foundational.

The problem is that what Reid considered to be common sense principles might not in fact be commonly held among all worldviews, and questioning their truth might very well be one of the roles of philosophy. While Reid affirmed that knowledge is possible, in contrast to Hume's skepticism, his view leads to a kind of fideism where certain beliefs are held as basic and not needing proof. The problem is that these beliefs are not agreed upon by every worldview, and in fact seem to differ from worldview to worldview, and thus the assertion of such beliefs without proof and in the face of challenges from other worldviews becomes fideistic. This leads to problems for Christianity because it does not affirm a clear general revelation and therefore cannot establish the inexcusability of unbelief or the need for redemption.

The German philosopher Immanuel Kant rejected Reid's response to Hume. Kant argued that the appeal to common sense is the means by which "the most superficial ranter can safely enter the lists with the most thorough thinker and hold his own . . . Seen clearly, it is but an appeal to the opinion of the multitude, of whose applause the philosopher is ashamed, while the popular charlatan glories and boasts in it."[20] For his part Reid admitted to being part of the popular view in saying, "on the one side stand all the vulgar, who are unpracticed in philosophical researches, and guided by the uncorrupted primary instincts of nature. On the other side stand all the philosophers, ancient and modern; every man, without exception, who reflects. In this division, to my great humiliation, I find myself classed with the vulgar."[21] Reid differentiated himself from earlier foundationalists by giving an expanded list of basic beliefs held by common sense. His concern was to establish certainty with respect to our knowledge of the real world, and he finds this in common sense beliefs that are only doubted by some "philosophers or crackpots." Kant's critique of Reid is insightful for some of Reid's common sense beliefs, but not all. If the law of non-contradiction makes the list, it seems that it does so not because it is the belief of the multitude, but because the opposite is literally not thinkable (this is how Aristotle spoke of this law). And this seems to be the criterion Reid gave for his common sense principles (they make thought itself possible), but whether each of Reid's common sense principles fulfills this criterion is a different question. A number of the beliefs Reid considered common sense might actually be beliefs that can be doubted, and have been doubted, and stand in need of proof. The law of non-contradiction cannot be doubted because it is necessary for any argument.

As for Princeton Theological the influence of Reid's thinking is reflected in the general attitude toward knowledge and the ability for all humans to know the same basic truths. The point here is not to show a specific connection between Reid and Princeton; other works have already attempted this. Instead the goal is to show that there is a similar affirmation. Both affirm that there are basic truths that all humans in all places can know, and that rationality itself assumes some specific principles the negation of which would stop all argumentation. Marsden said:

What view of faith and reason emerges from this evidentialist apologetic? On the face of it, it appears that these evidentialists thought that reason must play a very large role in support of faith. 'Without reason,' says Archibald Alexander of Princeton, 'there can be no religion: for in every step which we take, in examining the evidences of revelation, in interpreting its meaning, or in assenting to its doctrines, the exercise of this faculty is indispensable.' 'Reason is necessarily presupposed in every revelation,' echoed his famous student, Charles Hodge.[22]

Those skeptics who claim that reason cannot attain knowledge, or that there are no such universal principles, are assuming in their argument that argumentation is possible and that there is some standard for giving a sound argument. Hence Hodge and others presented their view as the only possible one because the opposite is self-refuting. In his *Systematic Theology* Charles Hodge clearly affirmed the role of reason. Christianity rejects rationalism in all of its forms, but it does not reject reason in the service of matters of religion.[23] In the first place, Hodge argued that reason is necessary in order to understand any other revelation.[24] Revelation is a communication of truth, and presupposes the capacity to receive it. "Truths, to be received as objects of faith, must be intellectually apprehended."[25] If a proposition is meaningless, however important it may be, it cannot be the object of faith. The objects of faith are beliefs such as the immortality of the soul, or that God is a spirit. In believing these a person is affirming their truth, and in so doing a person affirms that they understand what objects of faith mean. It follows that understanding is necessary and essential to faith. "The first and indispensable office of reason, therefore, in matters of faith, is the cognition, or intelligent apprehension of the truths proposed for our reception."[26]

Hodge concluded this section by saying, "about this there can be no dispute."[27] This is not a dogmatic assertion but a necessary truth. One cannot argue that argumentation is impossible. If a skeptic presents an argument that concludes reason is not able to apprehend meaning he would expect his audience to apprehend the meaning of his argument. In essence, such a person uses reason to deny reason. What is found in Hodge is the claim that reason, to give a minimal definition, is that by which a person comprehends the meaning of a proposition. This is different than apprehending the truth, and it is more basic than apprehending the truth (one must know what a statement means before being able to decide on its truth). Hodge here argues that reason is necessary for faith because in faith some proposition is believed, and in order to do this, reason must be used to understand what the proposition means. Hodge's *Systematic Theology* was used as the text at Princeton even in Warfield's time. Neither A.A. Hodge nor Warfield wrote their own systematics because there was no need. Thus Hodge's view of reason can be said to have been Princeton's view.

Princeton affirmed that God can be known through the use of reason. The next step is to see how the Princetonians viewed clarity. In what way is God's existence and nature known? Hodge's systematics will again be the most obvious source. In it he distinguished between three possible origins of the idea of God. The first is that the idea is innate, second that it is a deduction of reason, and third that it is a product of tradition.[28] He argued for the first against the last two. For the purposes here it is important to see what he meant by "innate idea" as opposed to a deduction of reason. Hodge defined innate as "that which is due to our constitution, as sentient, rational, and moral beings. It is opposed to knowledge founded on experience; to that obtained by *ab extra* instruction; and to that acquired by a process of research and reasoning."[29] Hodge argued that it cannot be doubted that there is such a knowledge, and that the mind is so constituted that it sees some things immediately in their own light.[30] In such cases, provided that a person understands what is meant, the truth will be grasped. These Hodge called intuitions, or primary truths, laws of belief, innate knowledge, or ideas.[31] To call a belief innate is to indicate its source. It does not imply that the mind is born with ideas, in terms of "'patterns, phantasms, or notions,' as Locke calls them."[32] What Hodge meant is that the mind is so constituted that it understands some things to be true without proof and without instruction.[33]

The law of non-contradiction is necessary for argumentation itself. The law of non-contradiction is the case because the opposite is impossible. Reason, specifically the law of non-contradiction, plays an essential part in thinking. Hodge called reason the *judicium contradictionis*.[34] Because faith, which is the believing of a doctrine to be true, involves the mind, it is not possible to have faith in a doctrine that is contrary to reason. In this way reason can judge what is and is not a special revelation. "We are, consequently, not only authorized, but required to pronounce anathema an apostle or angel from heaven, who should call upon us to receive as a revelation from God anything absurd, or wicked, or inconsistent with the intellectual or moral nature with which He has endowed us."[35] The mind of man is to be submitted to God, and this submission is absolute; what humans are submitting to is infinite wisdom and goodness. Hodge affirmed that it is impossble for God to contract himself, and equally impossible for him to declare as true, through special revelation of any kind, what he has made it impossible for humans to believe by the laws of our nature.[36]

It is not the case that reason and the impossible are whatever seem difficult to believe for the culture or a particular person. While the law of non-contradiction is not arbitrary, many times standards are set up that are arbitrary. "Men are prone to pronounce everything impossible which contradicts their settled convictions, their preconceptions or prejudices, or which is repugnant to their feelings."[37] Hodge gave as examples that the earth revolves on its axis and moves through space at a high speed. It is similar folly for men to reject the claims of Scriptures because they do not fit in with their previous assumptions about what is practically possible. "The impossible cannot be true; but reason in pronouncing a thing impossible must act rationally and not capriciously. Its judgments must be guided by principles which commend themselves to the common consciousness of men."[38] In the contemporary age it may seem "impossible" to many that God created the world in six days. Yet this is by no means impossible in terms of being a logical impossibility, and to declare it as such is to use a cultural standard instead of reason. In an important way Hodge's use of reason reflects how he and other Princetonians responded to the liberal scholarship of the 19th century. Concerning such trends as higher criticism, evolution, and comparative religions the Princetonians consistently pointed out that these are expressions of the materialist, or naturalist,[39] worldview (see Hodge's *What is Darwinism?*). These trends are not "scientific advancements" in the way that Newton's explanation of motion was. They are the cosmological expression of a worldview. Thus for a naturalist to claim that the creation account in Genesis is "irrational" is an example of begging the question, and the very kind of thing Hodge claimed is not a correct use of reason.

The role that Hodge gave to reason extends even to the judgment of special revelation. Hodge stated that reason is meant to judge special revelation. Such a revelation will not contain contradictions, and any revelation that does is not from God. It is reason's prerogative to judge the credibility of any revelation.[40] Reason judges what is impossible (that is impossible which contradicts itself), and this includes special revelation.[41] Hodge did not see this as setting a human standard to judge God. It was during this time (1800's) that "higher criticism" of the Bible became the popular trend in academic circles.[42] Yet the scholars who took part, and continue to take part, in that activity were not doing what Hodge outlined. The contradictions that Hodge was speaking of are not the contradictions such critics of the Bible look for. Hodge was speaking of metaphysical contradictions about being, while these critics look for what is "practically" difficult for their culture (worldview) to accept. When Hodge referred to reason he was not speaking about "what people commonly believe." He was particularly talking about the law of non-contradiction. He saw this as part of the standard for knowing that God Himself gave to man. Therefore it follows:

(1.) That is impossible which involves a contradiction; as, that a thing is and is not; that right is wrong, and wrong right. (2.) It is impossible that God should do, approve, or command what is morally wrong. (3.) It is impossible that He should require us to believe what contradicts any of the laws of belief which He has impressed upon our nature. (4.) It is impossible that one truth should contradict another. It is impossible, therefore, that God should reveal anything as true which contradicts any well authenticated truth, whether of intuition, experience, or previous revelation.

Men may abuse this prerogative of reason, as they abuse their free agency. But the prerogative itself is not to be denied. We have a right to reject as untrue whatever it is impossible that God should require us to believe. He can no more require us to believe what is absurd than to do what is wrong.[43]

For Hodge (and the Princetonians) there is, within Christian doctrine, no tension between reason and faith. People place faith in what they understand to be trustworthy, and understanding requires reason. Faith is not belief in what is absurd or self-contradictory. One does not have faith in square-circles, uncaused events, or that 2+2 is 5. One has faith in what is not seen, or even in what is practically impossible (vs logically impossible) like the parting of the Red Sea. But in the context of Moses and the Red

Sea the object of faith was that God would preserve His people which is consistent given the nature of God and his promise to Abraham. The objects of faith can thus be judged by reason. Hence faith in God requires that God's eternal power and divine nature can be known. Special revelation from God requires that there is a God. And so Hodge argued that God's eternal power and divine nature are known apart from special revelation. He asserted that all humans are bound by their very nature to believe in God, and that this cannot be avoided except through a derationalizing and demoralizing of their whole being.[44]

Hodge believed that the existence of God is obviously manifested, by the entire creation, so that belief in God's existence is a natural product of the use of reason, as part of our very nature.[45] This is to say that God's existence is readily knowable, or clear to reason. It is not a deduction arrived at only after strenuous reasoning. It is not only for those minds that are able to leap nimbly through abstract thoughts. It is clear to all minds, however well or poorly educated. Hodge rejected the idea that belief in the existence of God is the result of a long chain of deductive reasoning.[46] It is not a generalization of science, like the law of gravitation, which is assumed in order to explain a large amount of phenomena. God is more than a first cause of the universe. Such theories are possible only for cultivated minds, and hence cannot account for the idea of God, and the belief in Him, found in the minds of all humans, even those with no formal education.[47] It does not require a university degree in order to comprehend God's existence. Hodge's claim was that God's existence is so clear that it is basic to other beliefs and knowable by all that think.

For Hodge the Bible was not the beginning of apologetics or the belief in God. The Bible itself assumes God's existence, and its message of redemption assumes sin. This sin is at the basic level a rejection of God and his revelation in creation and providence. Hodge believed that there is sufficient proof (clarity) that God exists: "The Bible regards unbelief as a sin, and the great sin for which men will be condemned at the bar of God. This presumes that unbelief cannot arise from the want of appropriate and adequate evidence, but is to be referred to the wicked rejection of the truth notwithstanding the proof by which it is attended."[48] Hodge clarified that the claim that humans are not responsible for their faith arises from a confusion of ideas. Inexcusability does not apply to truths that are not clear, to speculative truths, or truths that require some matter of fact to know. "It is no sin not to believe that the earth moves round the sun, if one be ignorant of the fact or of the evidence of its truth."[49] But when unbelief is a sin, such unbelief has all the inexcusability that the sin brings with it.[50] Some beliefs can be maintained only by those having a reprobate mind, and that a person has such beliefs is evidence of their state.[51] The ignorance that humanity is inexcusable for having is ignorance of the eternal power and divine nature of God.

Princeton held that humanity could know God. It is unbelief that is unreasonable, not belief. And it is this unbelief that is inexcusable. This implies that it is clear that God exists so that humans are without excuse in their unbelief. It is in this sense that there is a Christian apologetic. It is in this sense that special revelation makes sense (as redemptive revelation). The above establishes the foundation for the rest of this study. It not only gives some sense of Princeton Theological's position with regards to general revelation, but it gives the direction that apologetics is to take. Those who ask others to place their belief in the irrational are not doing apologetics (in the Princetonian sense). One who depends on irrationalism cannot argue that others should place their belief in one kind of irrationalism rather than another kind of irrationalism without becoming self-referentially absurd. Similarly, those who claim that knowledge is not possible are not in a place to give an apologetic. Apologetics assumes that reason can be used to know God, that God's eternal power and divine nature are clear, that the failure to see what is clear makes a person inexcusable and in need of redemption. It is with this in mind that Warfield's view of apologetics will be investigated.

Notes

1. Mark Noll, "The Princeton Theology," *Reformed Theology in America*, ed. David Wells (Grand Rapids: Baker Books, 1997), 18.
2. Marion Ann Taylor, *The Old Testament in the Old Princeton School (1812-1929)* (San Francisco: Mellen Research University Press, 1992), 6.
3. Taylor, *The Old Testament*, 7.
4. Taylor, *The Old Testament*, 8.
5. Taylor, *The Old Testament*, 8.
6. Taylor, *The Old Testament*, 9.
7. Taylor, *The Old Testament*, 9.
8. Taylor, *The Old Testament*, 9.
9. Taylor, *The Old Testament*, 11.
10. Benjamin B. Warfield, "Introduction," in *Apologetics*, Francis Beattie (Richmond: Presbyterian Committee of Publication, 1903), 19-32. 24.
11. Noll, 21.
12. Noll, 22.
13. George Marsden, *Understanding Fundamentalism and Evangelicalism* (Grand Rapids: Eerdmans Publishing Company, 1991), 128.
14. Audi, 783.
15. George Marsden, "The Collapse of American Evangelical Academia," in *Faith and Rationality: Reason and Belief in God*, ed. Alvin Plantinga and Nicholas Wolterstorff (Notre Dame: University of Notre Dame Press, 1983), 224.
16. Marsden, "The Collapse," 224.
17. Marsden, "The Collapse," 225.
18. Reid, "Essays," 483.
19. Reid, "Essays," 480.
20. Kant, "Prolegomena," 535.
21. Reid, "Essays," 483.
22. George Marsden, "American Evangelical Scholarship," in *Rationality in the Calvinian Tradition*, ed. Hendrik Hart, Johan van der Hoeven, Nicholas Wolterstorff (Lanham, MD: University Press of America, c1983), 238.
23. Charles Hodge, *Systematic Theology*, (Massachusetts: Hendrickson Publishers, 1999). 49. Paul Kjoss Helseth writes against the view that the Princetonians were rationalists: "When Old Princeton's 'intellectualism' is interpreted within a context which affirms that the soul is a single unit that acts in all of its functions - its thinking, its feeling, and its willing - as a single substance, it becomes clear that the Princeton theologians were not cold, calculating rationalists." Paul Kjoss Helseth, "B B Warfield's Apologetical Appeal to 'Right Reason': Evidence of a 'Rather Bald Rationalism'?" in *Scottish Bulletin of Evangelical Theology* 16. (Autumn 1998): 156-177. 157.
24. Hodge, *Systematic*, 49.
25. Hodge, *Systematic*, 49.
26. Hodge, *Systematic*, 49.
27. Hodge, *Systematic*, 49.
28. Hodge, *Systematic*, 191.
29. Hodge, *Systematic*, 191.
30. Hodge, *Systematic*, 191.
31. Hodge, *Systematic*, 191.
32. Hodge, *Systematic*, 192.
33. Hodge, *Systematic*, 192.
34. Hodge, *Systematic*, 52.

35. Hodge, *Systematic*, 52.
36. Hodge, *Systematic*, 52.
37. Hodge, *Systematic*, 52.
38. Hodge, *Systematic*, 51.
39. Here defined as one who accepts only material causes as explanations for events.
40. Hodge, *Systematic*, 50.
41. Hodge, *Systematic*, 50.
42. Theodore P. Letis investigates the relationship between the German view of textual criticism and the Princetonians in his article "B.B. Warfield, Common-Sense Philosophy and Biblical Criticism." McClanahan in his article "Benjamin B. Warfield: Historian of Doctrine in Defense of Orthodoxy" argues that "Warfield and the Princetonians of his generation approved, introduced in some cases, and employed the principles of biblical criticism, though, one would say, conservatively." James S. McClanahan, "Benjamin B Warfield : Historian of Doctrine in Defense of Orthodoxy 1881-1921." *Affirmation* 6 (Fall 1993): 89-111.
43. Hodge, *Systematic*, 52.
44. Hodge, *Systematic*, 201.
45. Hodge, *Systematic*, 199.
46. Hodge, *Systematic*, 199.
47. Hodge, *Systematic*, 199.
48. Hodge, *Systematic*, 54.
49. Hodge, *Systematic*, 54.
50. Hodge, *Systematic*, 54.
51. Hodge, *Systematic*, 54.

# Chapter 2:
# Benjamin B. Warfield and Right Reason: The Clarity of General Revelation and Function of Apologetics

In B.B. Warfield[1] there is a continuation of Hodge's thinking on apologetics. Warfield never wrote a systematic theology of his own as Charles Hodge had already filled the need. Warfield was very prolific however, contributing articles and reviews on numerous topics. He upheld the Princeton ideas of Common Sense Realism in his view of apologetics and how God is known. His debate with Abraham Kuyper forced Warfield to better articulate his, and Princeton's, view. Warfield's view of apologetics includes his definition of apologetics (somewhat different from Kuyper's), his understanding of rationality and the ability to know God, his view of clarity and inexcusability, and finally his understanding of the role of special revelation. Here it will be argued that Warfield affirmed that there is a clear general revelation of God to all humans, that humans can know God through the use of reason, and that by implication unbelief is inexcusable. Much of this is stated explicitly by Warfield, although some of it will be draw out by implication. There are some problems that might arise due to an evidentialist influence in Warfield, and these will be considered in the conclusion.

Warfield defined apologetics in his *Studies in Theology*. Here he differentiated between apologetics and apologies. Apologies are defined as defenses of Christianity in some sense or another. Apologetics, however, is the establishment of the knowledge of God that Christianity professes to embody and endeavors to make efficient in the world.[2] Warfield did not see the essential function of apologetics to be a defense, in which case it would largely be defined by its opposition. Instead he defined apologetics as a constructive science that at times may need to defend itself but is largely concerned with the building of a system rooted in needs found in the human spirit. In this way it is not dependent on the reality of sin, but includes a knowledge that would have been important/necessary even if there had been no sin at all. It is in this context that Warfield made the claim "if it is incumbent on the believer to be able to give a reason for the faith that is in him, it is impossible for him to be a believer without a reason for the faith that is in him."[3]

Warfield firmly established the connection between the knowledge of God and apologetics, as well as faith and reason. The relationship between epistemology and metaphysics is particularly important because a thinker's epistemology will affect his metaphysics, and his metaphysics will affect his epistemology. The differences below between Warfield and Kuyper, and then Cornelius VanTil's attempt to find a third position, revolve around the question of the function of reason, and whether reason can be relative to a worldview (in contrast to being necessary for thought itself). It is something like this that Reid and the Common Sense Philosophers tried to hold. Reid may have mistakenly lumped many more things into the area of "common sense" than belonged there, but his aim was explicitly to find those fundamentals that are necessary for thought itself and hence cannot be doubted because they make thought possible.

That Warfield took a position very similar to Reid's (in contrast to Kuyper and VanTil) is an important aspect of Warfield's thinking on apologetics. Warfield was concerned with worldview apologetics. Warfield was concerned with the building of a system, but he does not give apologetics the role of proving every tenet of Christianity.[4] He saw this as a vulgar rationalism.[5] One important point for this book is that Warfield's epistemology cannot be said to be either rationalist or evidentialist.[6] Warfield claimed that evidence must be interpreted, and hence cannot stand on its own. He also did not attempt to prove Christianity by breaking it into atomic doctrines and then proving each of these. Instead, he saw the role of apologetics as establishing the whole of Christianity as the only true religion.[7] Warfield did not do this in an arbitrary fashion, stating that Christianity is true and hence so are its details. This would be to leave Christianity as the "great assumption", and simply beg the question with respect to its truth. Every worldview claims to be correct, and to be the only system that allows for knowledge. But this is much different than showing such to be the case. Instead he used a method similar to Reid's in that he appeals to "right reason" as the necessary precondition for knowing, and then shows how this reason necessarily reveals God. Warfield established clarity just on this point in that argumentation is not possible without reason, and reason reveals God to all. In this function apologetics lays a foundation on which theology is built, and the entire structure of theology is determined.[8] The function of apologetics is especially the establishment of a foundation on which the work of theology could be built.[9]

Warfield did not simply place two competing worldviews next to each other and argue that they cannot communicate, as did Kuyper. Warfield's appeal to reason followed that of Hodge outlined above. It is not so much that reason is neutral (the idea that VanTil levels his attack against) as it is that reason is necessary and is common ground for all humans. The unbelievers use the law of non-contradiction, but they use it in a limited way. The law of non-contradiction is necessary if argumentation is going to take place. A common method for arguing is to show that the opposite of a claim is impossible and hence the claim must be true. The use of this law shows that God exists. The opposite claims are self-contradictory. Hence reason is not neutral. However, the unbeliever does not use reason in this manner, and in neglecting to do so fails to know God. It is in this sense that Warfield claimed that the task of apologetics is to bring out clearly the reason for belief and to make its validity plain.[10]

Warfield was not claiming a neutral position where believer and unbeliever can meet. Reason is not neutral, and so the unbeliever is caught in a difficult position. If reason makes argumentation possible, then the unbeliever must recognize his need for reason. However, if reason also clearly and necessarily reveals God to the unbeliever, then he must accept this or give up reason. But to give up reason is to do so because of the either/or just mentioned, which is to say that to give up reason the unbeliever must use argumentation. But argumentation assumes reason, and so the unbeliever is left with a self-refuting position. There is no escape from reason.

Reason, while not neutral in one sense, is common ground because it is available to all humans. And, because reason reveals God's existence, there is a general revelation to all humans of God. All humanity can use reason to know God. Warfield explicitly states this when he asserts that the idea of God is a product of general revelation which can be known by all humans, and that it is not revealed by Scritpure but rather presupposed by Scritpure, as the foundation of the special revelation of God's grace to sinners.[11] The belief in God is a necessary belief because one must stop thinking (stop using reason) to avoid it. Warfield calls it an intuitive truth because it is an unavoidable belief.[12] If a person tries to understand anything at all, the starting point must be a realization of his own dependence.[13] This realization is coupled with the implication of there being one on who all else depends and who is therefore not dependent on anything.[14] This is a sort of immediate perception, and Warfield saw the theistic proofs as developing this idea further.[15] He seems to have relied on the arguments for a sufficient cause of the universe, an intelligent author of the order and design seen in nature, the necessity of an infinitely perfect being, and a moral absolute to establish a moral law for humans as dependent moral beings who are able to feel responsiblity and be conscious of moral problems.[16] We will consider some possible problems arising from his reliance on intuition and the theistic proofs in the conclusion of this work. However, the important point for consideration here is that Warfield believed it was both possible and necessary to give proof for God's existence and nature.

While Warfield does not speak explicitly about clarity, his position implies that reason reveals more than just the bare existence of God construed as an unmoved mover, or a "higher power." Rather, as the Apostle Paul says in Romans chapter 1, God's eternal power and divine nature are knowable from the things that have been made (the creation). This implies that reason necessarily leads a thinker to the idea of God if its implications are followed. In Charles Hodge's *Systematic Theology*, and A.A. Hodge's *Outlines of Theology*, there is a general kind of argument that attempts to categorize worldviews with respect to their claims about "being" and "dependence." Warfield appears to take a similar approach. This method of classification identifies three "kinds" of non-theistic worldviews. One that claims for matter the status of independence (material monism), one that claims for the self this status (spiritual monism), and then a dualism that tries a combination of both. The first, the materialists, wish to locate in matter the eternal cause of being, and limit all knowledge to material objects/causes. The second wish to find in the self the eternal cause of being, and hence explain all phenomena in terms of minds and ideas. The third tries a combination of the two with an emphasis on one or the other depending on the thinker: Plato emphasized the ideas/universals and Aristotle the objects/particulars. Such a brief look at these worldviews admittedly must simplify them. However the basic point is not lost: each tries to find what is "eternal" (independent/without beginning) in something other than God. That nothing can be said to be eternal except God is to say that each of these positions involves a self-contradiction.

The Princetonians claimed that reason shows that only God is eternal. It cannot be said of any other being that it is independent and eternal. Warfield affirmed that God is a personal Spirit, infinite, eternal, and unchanging in his being and in the attributes such as intelligence and will that belong to him as a personal spirit.[17] These attributes are known by humanity through general revelation, and are richly illustrated in special revelation.[18] The above concern with metaphysical views is something that the liberal Christianity of Warfield's day wished to avoid.[19] "Liberalism, one of the 19th century theological fruits of post-Kantian philosophy, wanted to rid Christian theology of its 'metaphysical' elements. To Warfield, this was apostasy."[20] For Warfield, and the Princetonians, an analysis of metaphysics was necessary because a thinker's metaphysical view will influence his interpretation of data and consequently his entire scientific approach.

In the above section are drawn out some of the good and necessary consequences of what Warfield said. For Warfield what can be known of God through general revelation is much more than a mere "higher power". It is a revelation of God as a Spirit, infinite, eternal, and unchanging in being, wisdom, power, holiness, justice, goodness, and truth (Westminster Shorter Catechism #4). This is a further development of proof for God's existence in that it does not stop with a "first cause" or the equally nebulous term "higher power." The argument used by the Princetonians (seen in both Charles and A.A. Hodge) is to point out the contradictions in all non-theistic claims and thereby establish theism (using the laws of excluded middle and non-contradiction). Again, this is something available to all humans, and thus all humans can come to a knowledge of God.

In light of the above it seems fair to say that Warfield believed in a clear general revelation of God's existence. His approach affirms that right reason reveals God. Hence all thinkers at all times can know God, and are responsible for knowing God. This is consistent with what is asserted in Psalm 19 and in Romans 1. The Psalmist says that the sun reveals God (Psalm 19). Thus, to worship it rather than its maker is an idolatry that can only be committed by not seeing what is clear to reason (that the creature is not the Creator). The clarity of God's existence and nature leads to inexcusability. If humans as rational beings can use reason to know God and yet fail to do so, there is no rational excuse for their unbelief. Warfield's apologetic argued that there is inexcusability for this unbelief. His approach to general revelation and knowing God are consistent with the claim that unbelief is inexcusable and requires redemption.

The Westminster Confession of Faith begins by saying: "the light of nature, and the works of creation and providence do so far manifest the goodness, wisdom, and power of God, as to leave men unexcusable" (Chapter 1). Thus, Warfield, following this tradition, preserved rationality, clarity, and inexcusability as essential features of apologetics. It is the denial or confusion of rationality, clarity, and inexcusability that leads to some of the problems in Kuyper's position that alarmed Warfield. It is also only in this light that the need for special revelation is seen. The Confession continues on to say: "yet are they [light of nature, creation, and providence] not sufficient to give that knowledge of God, and of his will, which is necessary unto salvation" (Chapter 1). Special revelation reveals how God will redeem humanity from sin. This assumes there is some sin that requires redemption. The sin of not seeing what is clearly revealed about God in general revelation is inexcusable and places humanity in need of redemption. Warfield affirmed this order between general and special revelation when he said that general revelation reveals the idea of God to all humans, while special revelation presupposes the idea of God and serves the purpose of communicating the grace of God to sinners.[21] This does not mean that humans as sinners can come to God through general revelation apart from special revelation, or can achieve redemption apart from special revelation. Rather, it affirms that special revelation is needed as a revelation about redemption because what can be known of God through general revelation has been ignored.

In Warfield's view general revelation reveals God's nature. However this revelation has been denied so that it can be said "none seek, none understand, and none do what is right." God's plan for redemption thus presupposes that there is sin that requires redemption. It is in this sense that Warfield says that special revelation is necessary. Special revelation is necessary to make known the plan of redemption that reveals the depths of the divine nature.[22] That knowledge which the Scriptures give cannot be replaced by general revelation.[23] But this does not mean that general revelation is somehow weakened or blurred after the fall. Reason still reveals God as necessarily as before, the issue is whether or not humans will use reason to know God.

With these essential features of Warfield's position in mind, his debate with Abraham Kuyper (and later Cornelius VanTil's assessment of the two) will serve to show that the differences between these thinkers can be best understood in terms of their ability to defend the claim that God's existence is clear to reason so that all humans are inexcusable in their unbelief.

Notes

1. Benjamin Breckinridge Warfield was born at Grasmere, Kentucky in 1851. He entered the College of New Jersey at Princeton in 1868, and graduated with highest honors in 1871. Before entering the Theological Seminary of the Presbyterian Church at Princeton in 1873 he spent some time traveling in Europe. He was licensed to preach in 1875, but shortly after this was married and then spent some time studying at Leipsic. In 1876 he began teaching at Western Theological Seminary. However, upon the death of A.A. Hodge he was called to teach at Princeton Theological, where he was a professor from 1877 until his death in 1921.
2. Warfield, *Studies*, 3.
3. Warfield, *Studies*, 4.
4. Warfield, *Studies*, 9.
5. Warfield, *Studies*, 9.
6. See Helseth's article titled: "B.B. Warfield's Apologetics Appeal to 'Right Reason': Evidence of a 'Rather Bald Rationalism'?" in which Helseth argues that the Princeton view should not be classified as rationalist.
7. Warfield, *Studies*, 9.
8. Warfield, *Studies*, 9.
9. Warfield, *Studies*, 4.
10. Warfield, *Studies*, 4.
11. Warfield, *Studies*, 109.
12. Warfield, *Studies*, 111.
13. Warfield, *Studies*, 111.
14. Warfield, *Studies*, 111.
15. Warfield, *Studies*, 111.
16. Warfield, *Studies*, 111.
17. Warfield, *Studies*, 111.
18. Warfield, *Studies*, 111.
19. James S. McClanahan, "Benjamin B Warfield : Historian of Doctrine in Defense of Orthodoxy 1881-1921," *Affirmation* 6, (Fall 1993): 89-111. 89.
20. McClanahan, "Benjamin", 89.
21. Warfield, *Studies*, 109.
22. Warfield, *Studies*, 110.
23. For a look at Warfield's relation to textual criticism see the articles by Letis and McClanahan mentioned above.

## Chapter 3:
## Benjamin B. Warfield and Abraham Kuyper: Worldview Relativism and the Question of First Principles

The relationship between B.B. Warfield and Abraham Kuyper[1] was one of mutual respect. Warfield was instrumental in getting Kuyper to give the Stone Lectures at Princeton in 1898, and then translating these into English. These lectures are now found in the volume titled *Lectures on Calvinism*. However, they disagreed on a number of significant points including apologetics. Although Kuyper did make important contributions to apologetics in terms of his analysis of worldviews, he did not maintain inexcusability precisely because he did not maintain a clear, general revelation or rationality that is able to know this revelation.

Warfield, in an introduction to Francis Beattie's *Apologetics*, took the time to address what he thought were the failings of Kuyper's view on apologetics. Warfield was specifically concerned with the small role Kuyper gave to apologetics:

> It is a standing matter of surprise to us that the brilliant school of Christian thinkers, on whose attitude towards Apologetics we have been animadverting, should be tempted to make little of Apologetics. When we read, for instance, the beautiful exposition of the relation of sin and regeneration to science which Dr. Kuyper has given us in his *Encyclopedia*, we cannot understand why he does not magnify, instead of minimizing, the value of Apologetics.[2]

Warfield saw the cause of this small role for apologetics in Kuyper's system as the distinct contrast Kuyper makes between "the two kinds of science."[3] The product of the sinful man is different in kind than the product of the regenerate thinker. This is the essential difference between these two thinkers, and at its center is the reality that Kuyper's system did not preserve rationality and clarity.

The role Kuyper assigned to apologetics followed from his view of epistemology in general. Thus it makes sense to look at how Kuyper built a theory of world and life views that makes apologetics, and reasoning (in one sense) helpless. The notion of "worldviews" is central to Kuyper's thinking. "This concept is so fundamental to his thought, so important to his career and so central to his international legacy that 'Kuyper' and 'worldview' are virtually inseparable."[4] The question becomes whether there is any similarity between the believer and unbeliever with respect to knowledge. "The epistemological question which lay at the heart of the division between Kuyper and Warfield was whether or not the acquisition of knowledge was exactly the same in principle for the regenerate and the unregenerate mind."[5] VanTil explained that Kuyper denied any point of neutrality between the Christian and the non-Christian that could be used as a point of contact for debate.[6] VanTil's development of Kuyper will be the focus later and so without going into his view it is relevant to note here that Kuyper (and VanTil) claimed that the only way a non-theist can know anything is by borrowing from the theistic worldview.[7]

Kuyper agreed with the Protestant tradition in saying that all that is known of God is from God's revelation to us. There is no beatific vision where God is seen directly apart from his work. "All knowledge of God must ever be the fruit of self-revelation on His side."[8] There is a difference between knowledge and belief. The unbelievers are in a state of believing propositions that are false. That is, they violate the standard/method for knowing. But, of course, they would not admit that they do this. The unbelievers, as well as the believers, both think that they are doing what it takes to gain knowledge. The former are incorrect about this, the latter are correct. In this sense there are two "kinds" of people. Kuyper divided them into those who admit of more than the natural world as a source of knowledge, and those who admit of only the natural realm:

> This naturally all falls away when you encounter a difference *of principle*, and when you come to deal with two kinds of people, i.e. with those who part company because of a difference which does not

find its origin within the circle of our human consciousness, but *outside* of it. And the Christian religion places before us just this supremely important fact. For it speaks of a regeneration, of a 'being begotten anew,' followed by an enlightening, which changes man in his very being; and that indeed by a change or a transformation which is effected by a supernatural cause.[9]

How can these two worldviews justify their starting points? Kuyper did not think this is an unfair question for one worldview to ask another.[10] He did, however, claim that one starting point cannot be used to judge another starting point.[11] The natural man, with his materialist assumptions, cannot judge the reliability of the theist and his assumptions (which for Kuyper are those found in special revelation).[12] This is essentially the way that the evolution/creation debate has been waged. The evolutionist will demand a material cause for all phenomena, and the creationist will insist that there are non-material causes that can account for the phenomena. Such a debate cannot be settled unless the issue of material/non-material causes is first decided.[13] These two cosmologies are parts of the worldviews Kuyper was speaking about. There is an "abyss in the universal human consciousness across which no bridge can be laid."[14] This abyss, for Kuyper, finds its origin in the regeneration that calls some from their sin to know God.[15] While Warfield agreed that it is necessary, in the fallen state, to be "reborn" in order to know God, this rebirth is a restoration of the use of reason in the person. Hence the apologist can use reason to show that the unbeliever's worldview has no consistency and in this way "demolish the strongholds" of the unbeliever. Kuyper, on the other hand, saw such argumentation as useless.[16] But Warfield did not see the role of the apologist as the one who gives life, which is the work of the Holy Spirit. It is the role of the apologist to speak the truth, to use reason against the unbeliever's worldview, and it is through these means that the Holy Spirit works.[17] While the Apostle Paul cannot give a new mind to fallen men, he can preach the Gospel in the hope that the Holy Spirit will use this work. And at Mars Hill in Athens the Apostle Paul addressed the Greek philosophers of his day by arguing that if they wish to understand life, motion, and being they must first understand God's existence (Acts 17:28). This difference with respect to the role of apologetics finds its beginning in a difference over the nature of reason. Kuyper's division of humanity into two groups leaves reason helpless.

Kuyper believed that these two kinds of people operate with different principles. The basic principles of a system determine the manner in which the system will be developed. This is similar to Reid's foundationalism. Each system has foundational principles. However, unlike Reid, Kuyper did not think that these are "common sense." These principles are not agreed upon by all humans. Actually, the fallen men have one set of principles, but the regenerate have a different set of principles. This results in two different standards for knowledge. In an important way this is a direct contradiction to Reid's common sense philosophy. Because all beliefs are relative to a worldview, there are no "common sense" beliefs that transcend all worldviews. There is no neutral position on which these two worldviews can agree. Kuyper's emphasis is that there are two kinds of people that are distinguished by their starting points.[18] These different starting points result in a different content rising from consciousness, a different point of view about the cosmos, and consequently different actions. For Kuyper this leads to two kinds of human life, and two kinds of science to support that life.[19] Thus any attempt to find a unity of science leads to a denial of the fact of palingenesis (rebirth), and consequently a denial of the Christian religion.[20]

The result of the two kinds of epistemologies is the division in "science" mentioned just above. Neither kind will admit that the other is really doing science because both operate with different principles that arrive at different conclusions. These principles are interpretive in that they are not derived from data but are used to understand the data. Hence there is no neutral data that can be referred to in order to prove one science is better than the other. Kuyper did not argue that there are two coherent explanations of the cosmos that can both explain what "is" with radically different representations.[21] He insists that truth is one, and hence science is really only one.[22] Kuyper did not mean that different scientists have arrived at different conclusions that contradict each other and hence cannot both be true. What he meant is that both the believer and the unbeliever, operating with different starting points, wish to investigate the object and in doing so wish to offer a systematized account of what exists.[23] There may seem to be a similarity between the two kinds of people, and they may even live together in unity to some extent. However the different starting points guarantee a difference in terms of method and inference. The conclusions arrived at will be influenced by the difference in method. In one sense this is a coherentist view of knowledge. The unbelievers arrive at knowledge by being consistent with their first principles. The same holds for the believers. But Kuyper did not want to admit that the unbelievers have knowledge in the sense of a true, justified belief. While their beliefs may be consistent with their first principles, they are not true because their first principles are not true. Hence the problem is in the principles. Kuyper said that whatever the formal similarities in their work, they are running in opposite directions because they have different starting points. And because of this difference they approach their work with different motivation and different perspectives about its purpose and goal. The difference in starting point affects the entire system that follows from the starting points, and results in a difference in all aspects of life.[24]

Kuyper did not argue that there is nothing in common between the two kinds of people. Everything is not a matter of worldview relativity. Some things, like weight, can be established by anyone who understands how to take a measurement. But it is the interpretation of data with respect to issues like cosmology that is important. The natural sciences are not only concerned with matters like weight, and it would be unfair to reduce them to this that seems to be the lowest part of their investigation.[25] Equally unfair would be to argue that the difference is so substantial that not even these sorts of studies (measurement) are in common.[26] Kuyper gave to perception an absolute character that transcends a person's worldview.[27] Such objects of knowledge are knowable by all humans at all times, but they hardly seem to be that for which humanity is inexcusable before God. In allowing for a common area of knowledge Kuyper gave some credence to Reid's view, and hence to Princeton: "it should be gratefully acknowledge that in the elementary parts of these studies there is a *common* realm, in which the difference between view - and starting-point does not enforce itself."[28]

It is the same with logic itself. Kuyper recognized that there is only one logic and not two different kinds of logic.[29] Hence there is some room for arguing that the unbelievers are not really following the "right reason." Involved in their unbelief is the denial of this logic that is not two, but one. But Kuyper used "logic" in a way that involves only inference between propositions. Thus logic cannot establish first principles in the way that reason (as the laws of thought) can. Logic only operates once there is a proposition from which to make a deduction. For Kuyper the two worldviews are contradictions. The naturalism of fallen man stands in contrast to the regenerate man who accepts special revelation from God, the Creator of the natural order. A person can be interested in science without being interested in studying the most fundamental principles of life. Kuyper saw that there are many aspects of science where details are studies, and awards can be won, without getting to the antithesis of the two worldviews. However, as this work is done it brings out more clearly the antithesis of the two worldviews.[30]

There is a similarity here between Kuyper and Plato's allegory of the cave (Republic 7.514). In this allegory the prisoner who escapes the cave and views things as they are is taken to be insane by those still in the cave. But the cave dwellers make this accusation because they have not used reason to understand the nature of things (represented in the allegory as the sun which illuminates the world). The prisoners in the cave do not know about the world as it is, only about the reflections and their inductions based on these. Kuyper's division within humanity is similar. The unbelievers have the capacity to understand how things are. The difference between the believers and unbelievers is a difference of attitude with respect to the use of reason. One has used reason, although he had to be given the desire to do so by God through regeneration, the other has not been regenerated and does not want to use reason. Thus there is a standard for objective knowledge and science, and the generic science follows this standard. Science, as Kuyper maintained, ought to follow some specific guidelines: He first assigned to it the investigation of nature and essence of God's revelation; second to analyze the material inferred from this; and third to explain how this material, including the revelation itself, relates to the intellectual life of man.[31]

Kuyper's two kinds of men form two kinds of theory. These are, roughly, the believer's worldview and the unbeliever's worldview. Kuyper further identified them as the Christian and the Modern views: "But, in deadly opposition to this Christian element, against the very Christian name, and against its salutiferoius influence in every sphere of life, the storm of Modernism has now arisen with violent intensity."[32] According to

Kuyper these two worldviews are at odds with one another. Both cannot be true, and both cannot be false. Notice the use here of the law of non-contradiction. This is almost not worth mentioning because of its universal application in such situations. It seems that Kuyper is unaware of his reliance on reason, and this makes his claim that there is nothing that both the believer and unbeliever must commonly accept in order to build a worldview doubtful.

The Modern worldview attacks Christianity and neither is reconcilable to the other. Kuyper saw this as a serious danger that imperiled Christianity. These two worldviews are wrestling with each other and in mortal combat. He defined Modernism as essentially naturalism, the view that only the material world exists and all knowledge must be derived from the material world. On the other hand, the Christian worldview recognizes God as the creator of the material world and sees the need for redemption through Christ.[33] The difference between the worldviews is a metaphysical difference. The Modern worldview looks to the then contemporary German pantheism that tried to locate the eternal in the universe itself.[34] In doing this God is reduced to the universe as a whole, and stripped of his title as Creator. Hence such a position is in no way compatible with Christian Theism, although part of the Modernist view is to try and reduce Christian Theism to naturalism. For Kuyper it was Protestantism alone that stood against the then prevailing views of Pantheism that he attributed to an ascendancy in German Philosophy and as responsible for the evolutionary theory of Darwin.[35] Such a worldview is in direct opposition to Christianity, and seeks to replace it with a "hopeless modern Buddhism."[36]

Notice that Kuyper locates only one worldview that stands in contrast to Christianity: the Modern, or materialist, worldview. This worldview is monistic in character, and attempts to reduce all being to matter. In contrast, it seems fair to say of Hinduism that while it is monist it attempts to reduce all being to self. Earlier there were outlined three non-theistic worldviews, titled the material monist, spiritual monism, and dualist. Kuyper did not deal with these last two, and his thinking on the issue seemed to be that if material monism was shown false then theism is true. However, there are other options beyond these two (VanTil makes the same mistake as will be seen below).

The Stone Lectures that Kuyper gave at Princeton in 1898 focused on Calvinism as a viable world and life view. The important point for Kuyper was to show first that Calvinism has all the characteristics of a world and life view, and second that it is a coherent world and life view. The importance of coherence rests on the importance given to the law of non-contradiction. If this law were avoidable, or jettisoned, coherence would lose all meaning. Kuyper's reliance on coherence, which to some extent is the method of proof for the correct worldview, demonstrates his need for this law, although it may not be a conscious part of his system. Kuyper's view of Calvinism is that it fulfills all the necessary conditions for a worldview. He placed it next to such "general systems of life" as Paganism, Islam, Roman Catholicism, and Modernism, in an attempt to show that Calvinism fulfills all the same conditions as these.[37] Further he argued that these conditions demand an explanation of the three fundamental relations of all human life, our relation to God, to man, and to the world.[38]

What makes Calvinism stand out is that it affirms that God is both transcendent and immanent. Only God is without beginning, and all else was made by God. In contrast the other worldviews try to find the eternal in some aspect of the creation. Kuyper contrasted Calvinism with Paganism, Roman Catholicism, and Islam. He believed that Paganism seeks God in the creation, Roman Catholicism posits a mediate communion between humanity and God, and Islam isolates God from the creation. Rather, Calvinism is based on the claim that while God is the creator, God also enters into the creation in order to have immediate (as opposed to mediate) fellowship with humanity.[39] It is the relationship of the creation to the Creator that is the defining point of every worldview. And Calvinism stands out as unique in this respect. This is what was pointed out above in contrast to material monism, spiritual monism, and dualism. It is theism that claims only God is eternal. And within theism Kuyper argued that only Calvinism consistently develops the view of God.

However, Kuyper's view does not seem to preserve the relationship between inexcusability and clarity. If there is not a clear general revelation of God, then it appears problematic for humanity to be held accountable for their failure to know God. Kuyper does affirm that there is a knowledge of God through general revelation (natural theology), but in a much different way than Warfield. Kuyper argued that: "Natural theology is with us no schema, but the knowledge of God itself, which still remains in the sinner and is still within his reach, entirely in harmony with the sense of Rom. i 19 *sq*. and Rom. ii 14 *sq*."[40] There is a knowledge of God that the sinner both possesses and refuses to admit that he possesses. There is a common grace that allows the sinner to exercise some of his capacity to know. But even this common grace reveals God in that if it were properly used the sinner would see his need for God.[41] Kuyper argued that even with the reality of sin there is a spark of light. Usually such metaphors (light) are used to explain reason, and so it seems fair to say that the unbeliever is left some use of reason. Even in the fallen state humans, if they used reason properly, could know God. If true this means that the problem is not with reason, but with the sinner.

Thus, for Kuyper, God's nature can be known through creation. Sin has dimmed man's ability to know, but not completely. What this means is central to this study. Unfortunately, it is ambiguous. How can reason be dimmed? It seems that either reason reveals God or it does not. And does this revelation get through? Does the sinner know God, and yet not know God? What does it mean to know God? Answering these questions will be important not only for Kuyper, but also for VanTil later in the study. Perhaps, it is the ambiguity here that causes the problems Warfield sees. Whatever the case, Kuyper's argument has the air of circularity about it: Kuyper stated there are two worldviews; he further said that these worldviews are contradictions of each other, and all reasoning by any person is relative to his first principles; this means that each worldview will reject the conclusions of the other worldview; however, this means that Kuyper's theory about there being two worldviews is relative to his worldview - most likely his opponents in the other worldview would not accept his view. How did Kuyper arrive at his conclusion? Did he do it in a way that is demonstrable to others in the contradictory worldview? If his claim that both worldviews cannot be true is based on the law of non-contradiction, is this a law of thought that the unbelievers would accept? Is the law of non-contradiction a "neutral" law that both sides can agree to? If so, Warfield's claim about right reason makes a good deal of sense. The difference between the two worldviews is a difference in the consistent use of reason. Reason, used properly, leads to only one worldview. The fallen man has beliefs that are ultimately contradictory to reason itself. Kuyper addressed this claim of circularity head on when he said:

> If the objection be raised that in the prosecution of science as directed by palingenesis, it is a matter of pre-assumption that there is a God, that a creation took place, that sin reigns, etc., we grant this readily, but in the same sense in which it is pre-assumed in all science that there is a human being, that human beings think, that it is possible for this human being to think mistakenly, etc., etc. He to whom these last-named things are not presuppositions, will not so much as put his hand to the plough in the field of science; and such is the case with him who does not know, with greater certainty than he knows his own existence, that God is his Creator.[42]

But what does Kuyper's view do for clarity? If it is clear that only one worldview is coherent, then to what extent are there really two worldviews? The difference is a difference with respect to the use of reason. One first principle is self-contradictory, the other is not. But Kuyper wanted "God" to be posited as a first principle in the way that the "common sense" ideas were for Reid. God makes argumentation possible, and should not be held up to "human standards" (including reason) by men. Kuyper saw this as a kind of reverence.[43] For a theologian to put himself in the place to investigate God is a reversal of the order. The result of this is the theologian who takes this approach either reverses the order of things and places the theologian as the critic of God, or falsifies the object of study and in the place of God puts religious phenomena. This second result might appear more innocent than the first, but Kuyper asserted that it results in a lack of the knowledge of God, which is essentially intellectual atheism.[44] This change in the focus of theology may have been a result of the Kantian influence. Kant argued that reason cannot know God, but rather that God must be postulated as a basis for morality. This means either that theology cannot be pursued as a science which uses reason to study God, or that the object of theology must be changed from God to something that can be known through reason such as religious experience or social history.

Even if there had been no sin to deter humanity in their seeking of God, Kuyper claimed that God's existence would not have been a matter of the believer's empirical investigations. Such investigations presuppose a worldview in which they are being interpreted. Thus, it is in theism that empirical investigations make sense. They cannot then be used to prove the theism that gave them their meaning. Kuyper believed that the knowledge of God must be imparted actively by God to the knower. This is true even had there been no sin. But with the reality of sin, humanity is not even able to receive the knowledge passively. God must change the human attitude, or "heart." In the sinful state humanity cannot come to know God without redemption given by God. This means that either the sinner will live without knowing God, or God must act to restore the sinner through redemption. This act of God is necessary in order to bring a sinner to the knowledge of God.[45] There is a temptation to claim that the clarity of general revelation is diminished due to sin. Kuyper may have said something like this. But the objective reality that reason reveals God does not change due to sin, rather sin is the failure to use reason to know God. Thus, it can be maintained both that general revelation is clear, and that humans as sinner do not see what should be seen. To affirm that general revelation is clear is not to affirm that sinners can achieve redemption apart from special revelation. Kuyper believed that sinners cannot come to know God apart from God acting in the sinners life, however he does not appear to affirm that general revelation is clear even after the fall, and this may be part of the reason he diminishes the role of apologetics.

The Christian claims that the sinner must be redeemed by God. The mind must be renewed by the power of God. Warfield agreed with this. But what does this mean with respect to clarity? Once dead in sin humanity does not care to know God and must be born again. But the state of being dead in sin is due to a failure to see what is clear in the first place. Hence, the continued state of death is a continued state of failure to see what is clear. And the being "born again" is a being returned back to the state of seeing what is clear about God. This does not seem to come out in Kuyper's view. Clarity has little place, and it seems hard to locate at best. This was Warfield's complaint, as will be seen below.[46] While the work of the Holy Spirit is necessary for re-birth, it is not necessary for the responsibility to believe in God.

But before Warfield's critique of Kuyper is examined, it is necessary to understand the role of special revelation in Kuyper's theory. For Kuyper, and later for VanTil, there is no possibility of knowledge apart from special revelation (Kantian influence). Kuyper argued that the indispensability of the Scriptures rests on: first, the necessity of the special principle given the weakening of the natural principle; second, that this special principle does not work atomistically to one individual, but to the whole human race (hence it is in written form).[47]

Kuyper developed the need for Scripture in a way that claims sin darkens man's understanding and leaves him without the ability to know. No knowledge of God is possible for fallen man apart from the Scriptures. The reality of sin is that no one is seeking God, and in this condition no one will know God. Thus without special revelation it is not possible for a person in the state of sin to know God.[48]

There are subtle nuances in this that must be handled with care. Warfield agreed that apart from regeneration none seek, none understand, and none do what is right. Regeneration is necessary for fallen man to come to know God. This regeneration accompanies the preaching of the Gospel found in the Scriptures. Yet, humanity is inexcusable precisely because, if they used reason, they could know God. "While reiterating the teaching of nature as to the existence and character of the personal Creator and Lord of all, the Scriptures lay their stress upon the grace or the undeserved love of God, as exhibited in His dealings with His sinful and wrath-deserving creatures."[49] The knowledge of God is available through general revelation, and the human failure to posses this knowledge leaves them in a miserable state before the justice of God.[50] This failure is sin. Humanity has a responsibility to believe in God apart from the work of the Holy Spirit. This difference provides a clear distinction between Kuyper and Warfield, and then, later, in VanTil as he argued against what he perceived to be weaknesses in Warfield.

The difference between Warfield and Kuyper is not a difference with respect to the effectual calling. Both agree that life is given only by the Holy Spirit. Instead it is an epistemological difference. Kuyper was more of a coherentist, while Warfield, following Scottish Common Sense Philosophy, was a foundationalist. Warfield's position was not that a person in the state of sin can come to know God through the work of apologetics. He affirmed that only through the redemptive work of God can the person who is dead in sin be brought to life in knowing God. However, he argued that faith is a form of conviction and is therefore grounded in evidence, and that evidence has its part to play in the conversion of the soul. Apologetics operates as an ordinary means both in the conversion of the individual and in the interaction between Christianity and non-Christian worldviews.[51] For Warfield this part was not a small part, nor was it a secondary or merely defensive part. He rejected the idea that its sole purpose was to protect Christians from the surrounding world, or to help the distracted Christian bring his intellect into conformity with his heart. Instead, Warfield saw the part that apologetics has to play as a central part in spreading the Gospel to the world and in addressing the challenges of non-Christian worldviews.[52] This implies that it is the duty of a Christian to use reason. As was noted above, Charles Hodge saw the fundamental job of reason as avoiding contradictions. Reason as the law of non-contradiction stands as judge over statements and systems. Where there is a contradiction, there cannot be truth (or meaning). This, for Warfield, was the distinction of Christianity. He believed that only Christianity can reason its way to dominion.[53] It is in this way that Christianity stands out from all other religions. It need not appeal to the sword, or seek some other way to extend itself. This means that the Christian has a duty to use reason.

With that in mind Warfield and Kuyper differ dramatically with respect to apologetics. The two kinds of men, and the resulting two kinds of science, that Kuyper spoke of are not completely rejected by Warfield. It seems essential to Christianity that there are believers and unbelievers, and that these two differ with respect to their worldviews. But what was rejected by Warfield is that there are two reasons, or two methods for knowing, that both result in a science. For Warfield the two sciences differ with respect to how consistent they are, they do not differ in kind. "There certainly do exist these 'two kinds of men' in the world - men under the unbroken sway of sin, and men who have been brought under the power of the palingenesis. And the produce of the investigation of these 'two kinds of men' will certainly give us 'two kinds of science'."[54] But Warfield insisted that this difference is not really a difference in kind, but is more a matter of corruption. "The depraved man neither thinks, nor feels, nor wills as he ought; and the products of his actions as a scientific thinker cannot possibly escape the influence of this everywhere operative destructive power."[55] Warfield argued with Kuyper in pointing out that the different sciences are affected in different degrees depending on the objects of their study.[56]

However, for Warfield the Christian worldview is the only rational worldview. All others reject reason at some basic point. A belief is basic to a worldview in that it explains that worldview's belief about what "being" is independent/eternal, and what "being" is dependent/temporal. If God as the Creator is denied this status, and some aspect of the universe (or the universe in its entirety) is viewed as eternal, then knowledge in others areas is not possible. "Without the knowledge of God it is not too much to say we know nothing rightly, so that the renunciation of the knowledge of God carries with it renunciation of all right knowledge."[57] Reason must be used consistently if it is to be used at all.[58] And this is the absurdity, rationally speaking, of the unbeliever's position. The unbeliever is being inconsistent at almost every point, and yet often times is claiming loudly to be using reason. Warfield argued that Christianity is not one of two worldviews, but the only worldview that is rational:

> We believe in Christ because it is rational to believe in him, not though it be irrational. Accordingly, our Reformed fathers always posited in the production of faith the presence of the '*argumentum propter quod credo*,' as well as the '*principium seu causa efficiens a quo ad credendum adducor.*' That is to say, for the birth of faith in the soul, it is just as essential that grounds of faith should be present to the mind as that the Giver of faith should act creatively upon the heart.[59]

The distinguishing mark of the Christian worldview is that the believer is able to know God as God has revealed Himself. This includes a knowledge from general revelation, and the use of reason itself to understand all revelation. The difference between the two worldviews is not a difference (or not only) with respect to special revelation. Kuyper gave apologetics a very small role because he thought reason cannot take the place of the Holy Spirit in giving new life. Warfield agreed about the Holy Spirit, but saw that there is a responsibility to know God apart from the work of the Holy Spirit, and the role of reason is one of the ordinary means that the Holy Spirit uses. Reason must be used even to understand the Scriptures, which are authoritative for the believer. In this Warfield differed dramatically from Kuyper and VanTil. He argued that while it is true that a Christian must take his stand in the Scriptures, he must first have these

Scriptures authenticated to him as such.⁶⁰ It is fair to ask which books really are Scriptures and which are not. Similarly, it is also true to say that Christianity is attained not by evidences and arguments but by a new birth.⁶¹ It is not within the power of arguments to make a Christian.⁶² "Paul may plant, and Apollos water; it is God alone who gives the increase."⁶³ It does not follow, however, that Paul should stop planting and Apollos stop watering. "Faith is the gift of God; but it does not in the least follow that the faith that God gives is an irrational faith, that is, a faith without grounds in right reason."⁶⁴

Thus there is a "common ground" that the believer can point to in speaking with the unbeliever. If knowledge is desired, this common ground cannot be denied. Taken as the laws of thought, reason is the common ground. Reason is not neutral in that it certainly reveals that there is a Creator. But reason is common in that all thinkers use it to some extent. In order to form a concept and express it in a word one must use the law of identity. Apart from this no word would be intelligible (Hodge gave the job of grasping meaning to reason). This means that there is only one body of knowledge, called science. This body of knowledge can be contributed to by the sinful human, although that contribution will not be what it could have been apart from sin. Warfield affirmed that the scientific work of the sinful human contributes a substantive part to the abstract science produced by what he called the ideal subject, although it is less valuable then it would have been without sin.⁶⁵

Warfield believed that it is the use of reason with respect to the only reasonable worldview that apologetics is concerned with. And apologetics can fulfill this function. He affirmed that the believer can show the unbeliever that the non-Christian worldview, first principles and all, is fundamentally inconsistent. At this point the unbeliever has only the option of giving up his worldview or giving up reason. For Warfield this gave a very important function to apologetics. Apologetics is not concerned with addressing how this particular argument or person can be induced to become a Christian.⁶⁶ It is concerned with something much more fundamental. It concerns itself with the actual establishment, "after a fashion valid for all normally working minds and for all ages of the world in its developing thought" of the basic facts that constitute Christianity.⁶⁷ Notice that "all normally working minds" sounds very similar to Reid, and reflects the influence of Scottish Common Sense Philosophy. The idea of "all normally working minds" is not that a poll be taken of all people to decide how people in fact try to get knowledge (mistakenly or otherwise). The idea is that there are some basic and necessary prerequisites for knowing, called reason, that are available to all men at all times. These can be used to establish the true system that, in virtue of being true, all men ought to believe. This gives to all the ability to know the Christian worldview, in a fundamental sense.

Warfield found the misapprehension of apologetics in a common duality among theologians, the antinomies of rationalism and mysticism. For Warfield the first is the attempt to find all knowledge through reason. This is rationalism. It claims to use reason and yet does not use reason fully because it fails to examine its assumptions. Rationalism denies the need for special revelation. The mystic, on the other hand, denies to reason any ability to gain knowledge. For the mystic, experience of the divine (usually a very ambiguous event) is the source of knowledge. For the mystic reason is unable to arrive at a knowledge of the divine. Hence: "To Rationalism, of course, Apologetics were an inanity; to Mysticism, an impertinence."[68] Wherever rationalism has been presupposed, there is proportionally a questioning of the validity of apologetics. And wherever mysticism has been presupposed, the use of apologetics is questioned and in general apologetics is distrusted.[69]

During Warfield's time, and most likely during the present as well, the rationalist principle was the most common. "At the present moment, the Rationalistic tendency is perhaps most active . . . where religion is supposed to seek and find expression only in value-judgments - the subjective product of the human soul in its struggle after personal freedom - and thus to stand out of all relation with theoretical knowledge, there, obviously, there is no place for a vindication of Christian faith to reason and no possibility of Apologetics."[70] Rationalism seeks coherence while working within the fallen principles. This is not the same as the use of reason to know God. Rationalism assumes principles that are at the outset self-contradictory (those of the natural man), and then deduces from these conclusions that are contradictory to the Christian world and life view. An example is Modernism and its cosmology of evolution. It assumes that matter can account for itself without reference to a Creator. Beginning with this assumption, it uses reason as a deductive method to draw out implications. These implications are consistent with its assumptions, but those assumptions may themselves be contrary to reason. Thus, a fault of rationalism is that it does not use reason fully enough. It uses reason constructively by building on assumptions, but does not use it critically to examine those assumptions.

This misuse of reason leads many, like Kuyper, to abandon reason altogether.

> The mystical tendency is showing itself in our day most markedly in a widespread inclination to decline Apologetics in favor or the so-called *testimonium Spiritus Sancti*. The convictions of the Christian man, we are told, are not the product of reasons addressed to his intellect, but are the immediate creation of the Holy Spirit in his heart. Therefore, it is intimated, we can not only do very well without these reasons, but it is something very like sacrilege to attend to them. Apologetics, accordingly, is not merely useless, but may even become noxious, because tending to substitute a barren intellectualism for a vital faith.[71]

In this view one will become committed by experiencing for himself that the worldview in question is beneficial. Of course, this is problematic because what counts as "beneficial" depends on a person's worldview. This (Kuyper's view of apologetics) was Warfield's main complaint against Kuyper. Apologetics was not abolished altogether by Kuyper, but it was given a subordinate role, as a subdivision of a subdivision of the "Dogmatological Group" where it is given the task of defending Christianity from philosophy (narrowly defined).[72] For all of the other significant contributions that Kuyper made, his view of reason, and consequently apologetics, left Christianity as the great assumption. Why pick Christianity over another view? Warfield believed that those who follow Kuyper's thinking will say that one should pick it because they have experienced that it is good. They have tried it out for themselves (in a manner of speaking) and seen that it works.[73]

Kuyper's role for apologetics was not to abolish it, but to give it a job of little importance. This follows from Kuyper's view of reason. Reason is incompetent with respect to convincing others. The two worldviews produce two kinds of men that cannot speak to each other about first principles. Warfield argued against Kuyper by vindicating reason itself. While the Scriptures are the source of theology, they themselves must be understood by reason. Reason helps a person to understand what the Scriptures are, and what they mean. Hence to posit them as a first principle is incorrect. Reason can be used to show that God exists, and it is used to understand God's special revelation with respect to redemption. This point about reason is the basic difference between Warfield and Kuyper. Warfield admitted that there are many attractive aspects to Kuyper's development of the theological sciences.[74] However, he saw it as a mistake to make the Scriptures the basic principle of knowledge.[75] Warfield argued that the Scriptures are not the object of theology, but its source.[76] Its object being the knowledge of God, and this must be shown to be in the Scriptures. However, before this can happen, it must be shown that there is a knowledge of God in the world, and previous to this is that there is a knowledge of God possible to man.[77] And before this it must be shown that there is a God to know, and with this line of thought Warfield argued that it is necessary to argue back to first principles.[78] These first principles are the realm of an apologetical theology, and this of necessity stands in the first place among the essential theological disciplines.[79] Because knowing God is the highest use of the human mind, and it is fundamental to all of life, any attempt to do science apart from God will be fatally incomplete.[80] The role Kuyper assigned to reason cannot be understood apart from his view of knowledge itself. Because Warfield and Kuyper differed with respect to knowledge, it comes as no surprise that they differ with respect to the role of apologetics.

Warfield's position with respect to reason and consequently apologetics is made clearer by contrasting it with Kuyper's. Kuyper's worldview relativism correctly pointed out the importance of first principles to a system. Warfield did not disagree with this. Kuyper also pointed out that these systems produce conclusions that are relative to their first principles. Again, Warfield agreed. However, Kuyper's view makes it impossible to judge between first principles. To some extent this is a defect in Reid's philosophy. It must be established, of each "common sense principle," that argumentation really is impossible if the principle were violated. The failure to do this is one contributing factor in the Common Sense Philosophy losing popularity. This loss in popularity is most likely due to the fideistic tendencies of Common Sense Philosophy.

However, if reason is defined narrowly as Charles Hodge mentioned above, are there really two reasonable first principles (theism vs. naturalism)? Are not the modernist's first principles self-contradictory? If so, the problem is with the use of reason. The correct use of reason at the basic level reveals that God is the Creator of the heavens and the earth and is owed whatsoever worship He desires from men. This approach states that humanity can use reason to know God, and can use reason to know that the opposite of the belief in God is self-contradictory (not possible).[81]

From here it makes sense to turn to Warfield's legacy. Specific attention will be given to Cornelius VanTil who accepted a position at Princeton in the years following Warfield's death, and was among the founding professors at Westminster Theological Seminary. VanTil is chosen because he was the shaping influence in apologetics at Westminster, and because he consciously tried to find a third position between Warfield and Kuyper. Many of VanTil's criticisms of Warfield revolved around the idea that reason cannot be used to judge God, and hence it is necessary to keep in mind Warfield's view of reason while proceeding.

## Notes

1. Abraham Kuyper was born in 1837 in Maassluis, a seaport town in the Netherlands. In 1855 Kuyper entered the university of Leiden. After this Kuyper spent some time in the ministry, until 1874 when he was elected to the Second Chamber and began his career in politics. Between 1880 and 1901 he taught theology at a university he had helped to found - the Free University of Amsterdam. In 1901-1905 he rose to be prime minister in the second Antirevolutionary Cabinet. In 1898 he was the guest speaker at the Stone Lectures at Princeton where he gave what have come to be known as his *Lectures on Calvinism*.
2. Warfield, "Introduction," in *Apologetics*, 27.
3. Warfield, "Introduction," in *Apologetics*, 27.
4. Peter S Heslam, "Architects of Evangelical Intellectual Thought: Abraham Kuyper and Benjamin Warfield," *Themelios* 24, no. 2 (Fall 1999): 3-20.
5. Heslam, "Architects."
6. VanTil, Cornelius, *Defense of the Faith* (Phillipsburg: Presbyterian and Reformed Publishing, 1967), 151.
7. VanTil, *Defense*, 151.
8. Kuyper, Abraham, *Principles of Sacred Theology* (Grand Rapids: Baker Book House, 1980), 348.
9. Kuyper, *Principles*, 151.
10. Kuyper, *Principles*, 381.
11. Kuyper, *Principles*, 381.
12. Kuyper, *Principles*, 381.
13. Donald Fuller and Richard Gardiner locate this as the issue when they say "with the 'death' of classical, *metaphysical* 'first principles of reason' in the nineteenth century due to Hume and Kant, empiricist and transcendental philosophers of science (despite differences) agreed generally in proposing some type of *physical* or naturalistic 'first principle' as the ground for the veracity of their scientific inquiry. That physical 'first principle' was ultimately grounded in this assumption of the uniformity of nature . . . Kant's own transcendental philosophy of science is dependent on this assumption" (Donald Fuller and Richard Gardiner, "Reformed Theology at Princeton and Amsterdam in the Late Nineteenth Century: A Reappraisal," *Presbyterion* 21 (Spring 1995): 89-117. 93.
14. Kuyper, *Principles*, 152.
15. Kuyper, *Principles*, 152.
16. Heslam, "Architects."
17. "While Warfield acknowledged that 'rational arguments can of themselves produce nothing more than "historical faith"', he nonetheless insisted that 'historical faith' is 'of no little use in the world' because what the Holy Spirit does in the new birth is not to work 'a ready-made faith, rooted in nothing and clinging without reason to its object', but rather 'to give to a faith which naturally grows out of the proper grounds of faith, that peculiar quality which makes it saving faith'. Since the Holy Spirit 'does not produce faith without grounds', we can infer that Warfield engaged in apologetics not to argue the unregenerate into the kingdom of God, but rather to facilitate their engagement in the most basic activity of human existence, namely reaction to the truth of God that is reflected into the soul" (Helseth, Paul Kjoss, "B B Warfield's Apologetical Appeal to 'Right Reason': Evidence of a 'Rather Bald Rationalism'?", *Scottish Bulletin of Evangelical Theology* 16 (Autumn 1998): 156-177. 177.
18. Kuyper, *Principles*, 154.

19. Kuyper, *Principles*, 154.
20. Kuyper, *Principles*, 154.
21. Kuyper, *Principles*, 155.
22. Kuyper, *Principles*, 155.
23. Kuyper, *Principles*, 155.
24. Kuyper, *Principles*, 155.
25. Kuyper, *Principles*, 157.
26. Kuyper, *Principles*, 157.
27. Kuyper, *Principles*, 157.
28. Kuyper, *Principles*, 158.
29. Kuyper, *Principles*, 159.
30. Kuyper, *Principles*, 166.
31. Kuyper, *Principles*, 172.
32. Abraham Kuyper, *Lectures on Calvinism*. Grand Rapids: Eerdmans Publishing Company, 1999. 10.
33. Kuyper, *Lectures*, 11.
34. Kuyper, *Lectures*, 18.
35. Kuyper, *Lectures*, 18.
36. Kuyper, *Lectures*, 18.
37. Kuyper, *Lectures*, 19.
38. Kuyper, *Lectures*, 19.
39. Kuyper, *Lectures*, 21.
40. Kuyper, *Principles*, 302.
41. Kuyper, *Principles*, 302.
42. Kuyper, *Principles*, 175.
43. Kuyper, *Principles*, 342.
44. Kuyper, *Principles*, 342.
45. Kuyper, *Principles*, 345.
46. A problem arises for Kuyper when his theory is applied to itself. Kuyper's theory is relative to his worldview, to his science, and hence is not universal, and one must wonder why it should be accepted. Why accept Kuyper's view over the other? Are there any universal/necessary truths? If there are, is not there really only one science, the correct one that uses these truths, and then a whole bunch of bad science? People might try to argue against the laws of thought, but "can" they argue against them? Warfield's view of right reason avoided these sorts of problems.
47. Kuyper, *Principles*, 405.
48. Kuyper, *Principles*, 249.
49. Warfield, *Studies*, 111.
50. Warfield, *Studies*, 111.
51. Warfield, "Introduction," in *Apologetics*, 19.
52. Warfield, "Introduction," in *Apologetics*, 26.
53. Warfield, "Introduction," in *Apologetics*, 26.
54. Warfield, "Introduction," in *Apologetics*, 27.
55. Warfield, "Introduction," in *Apologetics*, 27.
56. Warfield, "Introduction," in *Apologetics*, 27.
57. Warfield, *Studies*, 97.
58. Warfield, *Studies*, 104.
59. Warfield, "Introduction," in *Apologetics*, 25.
60. Warfield, "Introduction," in *Apologetics*, 25.
61. Warfield, "Introduction," in *Apologetics*, 25.
62. Warfield, "Introduction," in *Apologetics*, 25.

63. Warfield, "Introduction," in *Apologetics*, 25.
64. Warfield, "Introduction," in *Apologetics*, 25.
65. Warfield, "Introduction," in *Apologetics*, 27.
66. Warfield, "Introduction," in *Apologetics*, 32.
67. Warfield, "Introduction," in *Apologetics*, 32.
68. Warfield, "Introduction," in *Apologetics*, 20.
69. Warfield, "Introduction," in *Apologetics*, 20.
70. Warfield, "Introduction," in *Apologetics*, 20.
71. Warfield, "Introduction," in *Apologetics*, 20.
72. Warfield, "Introduction," in *Apologetics*, 21.
73. Warfield, "Introduction," in *Apologetics*, 21.
74. Warfield, "Introduction," in *Apologetics*, 24.
75. Warfield, "Introduction," in *Apologetics*, 24.
76. Warfield, "Introduction," in *Apologetics*, 24.
77. Warfield, "Introduction," in *Apologetics*, 24.
78. Warfield, "Introduction," in *Apologetics*, 24.
79. Warfield, "Introduction," in *Apologetics*, 24.
80. Warfield, *Studies*, 97.
81. Donald Fuller and Richard Gardiner summarize this difference when they say that Old School Princeton maintained a commitment to the pre-Enlightenment orthodoxy and its theological worldview, affirming the importance of reason as a metaphysical first principle, while the Amsterdam school accepted an anthropocentric Kantian worldivew and a theology more affected by Fichtian science than by classical Christian orthodoxy. (Fuller, "Reformed," 104).

## Chapter 4:
## Benjamin B. Warfield and Cornelius VanTil: Westminster Theological Seminary and the Presuppositional Apologetics of Cornelius VanTil

B.B. Warfield's legacy is not simple, nor does the following purport to make it seem that way. However, because Westminster Theological Seminary explicitly claimed to continue the tradition of the Old School Princeton Theology it makes sense to look there for a continuation of Warfield's method. And, because the present focus is on apologetics, it makes sense to look at Cornelius VanTil, who taught at Princeton Theological, was one of the founding professors at Westminster, and who developed the apologetical system that characterizes this seminary and is known as "Presuppositional Apologetics." While VanTil tried to avoid what he saw as mistakes in both Warfield and Kuyper, he replaced reason with special revelation, and did not explain clarity in a way to maintain inexcusability. Therefore, it will be argued that VanTil departed enough from Warfield's concept of "right reason" to do harm to the attempt of the apologist to show the inexcusability of all unbelief.

The changes at Princeton Theological Seminary and the beginning of Westminster Theological and the Orthodox Presbyterian Church revolved largely around J. Gresham Machen (1881-1937). It was Machen's concern for consistency with respect to the historic Church that led him and others to leave Princeton. W. Stanford Reid said:

> Although in 1926 the Directors wanted him [J. Gresham Machen] to become professor of apologetics, a move to which he was not much inclined, the Trustees, led by the president, J. Ross Stevenson, were opposed. The result was a battle that led to the reorganization of the administration: the Board of Directors was abolished and full control

of the school was given to a single Board of Trustees to which two signers of the liberal Auburn Affirmation were appointed. The resulting conflict between Machen and the new administration led to his resignation from the seminary in June 1929, on the ground that Princeton had now left its historic theological position.[1]

It was in this context that Westminster Theological was established, as an attempt to preserve what Princeton had been. When Machen left Princeton, a number of others also did who agreed that the historic creeds of the faith summed up true Christian doctrine and should not be departed from in favor of what Machen and others viewed to be compromises with non-Christian worldviews. When Machen left others also decided to leave. As a result they formed a committee to establish a new seminary named Westminster, located in Philadelphia, as an independent institution in the fall of 1929. In his opening address at Westminster Theological Seminary, Machen emphasized two aspects of its constitution. The first was the final authority of the Bible, which he said should be read as meaning exactly what it says. The second was that Princeton was lost to the cause of evangelicalism, and that Westminster would stand firmly in the Reformed theological position as expressed in the Westminster Confession of Faith.[2]

Because of VanTil's presence at Princeton, and his role at Westminster, his view is important for this work. Particularly of concern is his view of apologetics and how it represented both the Princeton tradition, and Warfield particularly, as well as Kuyper's position. VanTil attempted to formulate a third position that takes the best of both of these, and yet avoids what he saw as weaknesses in each. Some, like R.C. Sproul, accuse VanTil of being a Kuyperian (see Sproul's *Classical Apologetics*). But students of VanTil, like Greg Bahnsen, deny this and point to explicit statements by VanTil to the contrary (see Bahnsen's *VanTil's Apologetics: Reading and Analysis*). Here the concern is not with settling this matter so much as it is with understanding VanTil's epistemology and its affect on his apologetical system. VanTil relied heavily on the notion of a transcendental reason expounded by Kant. This had a defining affect on his system.

VanTil defined apologetics as: "the vindication of the Christian philosophy of life against the various forms of the non-Christian philosophy of life."[3] Like Warfield, VanTil saw the crux of apologetics in the proof of the theistic God's existence. He contrasted this with the "evidences" that are used to prove other truths of Christianity. Although VanTil's system is presuppositional, in contrast to evidential, he did not deny that evidences have a place in proof. VanTil distinguished between apologetics as giving proofs for theism, and evidences giving proofs for Christianity.[4] That is, apologetics deals with philosophy while evidences deal with facts.[5] And because apologetics deals with philosophy, specifically with establishing the foundation, it also deals with how evidences are to be interpreted. The interpretation of a given "evidence" is an essential part for that evidence playing a role in an argument or proof. Evidences by themselves are not enough to prove Christianity. Evidences must be interpreted to be given meaning, and hence what a specific "fact" means will depend on one's world and life view. VanTil gave an example of this:

> It is impossible and useless to seek to vindicate Christianity as a historical religion by a discussion of facts only. Suppose we assert that Christ arose from the grave. We assert further that his resurrection proves his divinity. This is the nerve of the 'historical argument' for Christianity. Yet a pragmatic philosopher will refuse to follow this line of reasoning. Granted he allows that Christ actually arose from the grave, he will say that this proves nothing more than that something very unusual took place in the case of 'that man Jesus.' The philosophy of the pragmatist is to the effect that everything in this universe is unrelated and that such a fact as the resurrection of Jesus, granted it were a fact, would have no significance for us who live two thousand years after him. It is apparent from this that if we would really defend Christianity as an historical religion we must at the same time defend the theism upon which Christianity is based. This involves us in philosophical discussion.[6]

The aim of apologetics is to demonstrate the truth of theism while showing that all other worldviews are false. Of course this is not derived exclusively from either Warfield or Kuyper since both saw apologetics as having this goal. Both Charles Hodge and A.A. Hodge included sections demonstrating the inconsistency of all non-theistic worldviews. And this certainly does seem to be the general aim of apologetics. Hence, it is no surprise when Greg Bahnsen said of VanTil that the latter viewed apologetics as the defense of the Christian faith by answering all the variety of challenges brought against it by unbelievers.[7] The Christian apologist establishes Christianity as the true worldview, over and against all non-Christian philosophies of life.[8] This is certainly in-line with the Princeton approach, as well as Kuyper's approach.

The uniqueness of VanTil appears when consideration is given to his epistemology. In this he did differ to some extent from Warfield and Kuyper, at least in his reliance on Kant. What Kant called a Copernican revolution in philosophy, VanTil called a Copernican revolution in apologetics. The revolution deals with a change from attempting to conform the mind to the world, to realizing that the world must conform to the mind. There are, for Kant, *a priori* principles through which all information is interpreted by the mind.[9] Hence, there is no way to "get at" the world apart from these, all that is available is the data once it has gone through the formal structure of the mind. In a way, this is to say that there are necessary preconditions for knowing, reasoning, and argumentation (as was seem in Reid earlier). Interestingly, for nineteenth century positivism, Kant's Copernican revolution entailed that "metaphysical views are no longer tenable."[10] This reliance on Kant has been traced to the Dutch Reformed tradition. Donald Fuller and Richard Gardiner argue, "it was the Dutch Neo-Calvinist Abraham Kuyper (as well as the Neo-orthodox generally) who, in fact, yielded to 'Enlightenment' views of metaphysics, science, and theology. It is our contention that while Old Princeton maintained and championed a pre-Kantian theological method, the Dutch Neo-Calvinist theologians reshaped Reformed theology to fit the mold of the Kantian worldview and a distinctively modern philosophy of science."[11]

Greg Bahnsen claimed that this presuppositional approach is one of the most important contributions given by VanTil. "One of the distinctive insights that VanTil has given to presuppositional apologetics is that every line of reasoning that is exalted against the knowledge of God, and every kind of objection or challenge to the faith that is raised by unbelievers, arises from an attitude of the heart and within the intellectual context of a world-and-life view."[12] Rather than argue against evolution *per se*, or against Marx's view of history, or Freud's view of man, the apologist must argue against the atheism/naturalism that are behind these. Each of these thinkers (Darwin, Marx, and Freud) assumes naturalism, and assumes that the Christian view is incorrect. Hence they are not "objective", or "neutral", as they would like to appear, but are very much saturated with assumptions that lead necessarily to the conclusions they draw. They may be internally consistent, but the question becomes whether their first principles, their presuppositions, are coherent. The presuppositions of a worldview affect every other part of the worldview, and consequently the entire outlook of the person. It is because of this that every encounter between worldviews is ultimately a conflict between their presuppositions. Thus, every apologetical encounter is a conflict between conflicting worldviews.[13]

VanTil, like Kuyper, located a basic non-Christian principle that is behind the fallen world and life view. This principle places humans as the source of knowledge, and elevates human "reason" to the place where God is for the Christian. Here there will be some ambiguities that arise because the term "reason" is sometimes used to refer to what are clearly the non-Christian naturalistic assumptions, which are by no means self-evidently true. At other times a method much like Charles Hodge's will be used in terms of reason as the law of non-contradiction. So VanTil's denial of the fallen man's ability to achieve knowledge through his own "reason" seems best defined not as the law of non-contradiction, but as a deductive/inductive method based on naturalism that produces such cosmologies as evolution and the oscillating universe theory. These are relative to their naturalist assumptions and hence cannot be true if naturalism is not true. In terms of his reliance of first principles VanTil bears similarity to Kuyper. VanTil also affirmed that the most basic assumption of the non-Christian worldview is that humanity, rather than God, is the final reference point in predication. VanTil thought that the idea of truth as an abstract entity disconnected it from God, and was therefore based on the non-Christian assumption.[14] For VanTil this meant that there can be no neutral place, or common ground, between the Christian and non-Christian. Whether a neutral place and common ground are to be equated was not questioned.

VanTil located the fallen human's assumptions as essentially placing humanity at the center. It is the job of the Apologist to challenge this notion. Can such a starting point really end up in knowledge? VanTil argued that it cannot, and that this is what the Reformed Apologist must point out. The Reformed Apologist must challenge this starting point in everything that the unbeliever says about anything.[15] It is this assumption that the "natural man" uses to interpret everything that is presented to him. In this sense it should be no wonder that the natural man rejects creation as an account of the origin of life. It is not because he is more "scientific" than the believer. It is because the natural man is confined to look for the cause of what he sees in the material world itself, rather than in the Creator of that world. This approach to apologetics tests basic beliefs for meaning.

VanTil called this method "presuppositional", and this name has come to characterize his apologetical system. In arguing presuppositionally the apologist locates and challenges the first principle, or most basic belief, on which the non-Christian view hinges. All views have presuppositions. "Everybody thinks and reasons in terms of a broad and fundamental understanding of the nature of reality, of how we know and of how we should live our lives."[16] This establishes how the apologist will approach argumentation against non-theistic worldviews. "To argue by presupposition is to indicate what are the epistemological and metaphysical principles that underlie and control one's method."[17] VanTil claimed that the presupposition for Christianity is the ontological Trinity, and this ultimately controls the Christian methodology.[18] The isolation of a system's basic assumption and the consequent evaluation of that assumption is not a unique characteristic of VanTil. What is important are the beliefs VanTil saw as being basic to a system.

The "transcendental argument" is another central feature to VanTil's apologetic. The argument is essentially that no arguments are possible apart from theism. It is only in the theistic worldview that argumentation makes sense. VanTil argued that the unbeliever cannot have any knowledge without being untrue to his presuppositions. It is only the theistic worldview that can consistently explain knowledge, science, morality, and everything else. Thus, it is either the case that the unbeliever does not know what he claims to know, or that the unbeliever does have knowledge but only because in this instance he is borrowing theistic principles to gain knowledge. If the unbeliever were consistent to his naturalism, knowledge would not be possible. The unbeliever tries to claim that logic, science, and morality are on his side against the Christian.[19] VanTil answered this by arguing that these are only possible within the Christian worldview, and only Christianity can rescue them from meaninglessness.[20] VanTil's challenge to the unbeliever was guided by the assumption that only Christianity provides the framework in which human reasoning and knowledge are possible.[21] This is called a "transcendental" defense of Christianity.[22] It is called "transcendental" because it argues for those principles necessary for any argumentation. Any attempt for a human to reason, and even reason and reasoning itself, are incoherent unless the truth of the Christian Scriptures is assumed, or presupposed.[23]

In the above is the ambiguity about the definition of "reason" mentioned earlier. VanTil claimed that man's reasoning is unintelligible unless the Christian Scriptures are presupposed. For the purposes here this is important in terms of the definition of "reason", as well as for what it does to the clarity of general revelation. If "reason" is taken to be the contemporary popular assumptions, then such assumptions as these are cultural and conventional. Different people, in different places, at different times, claim to "know" statements that contradict each other. Widespread belief is by no means knowledge. That our culture takes for granted the truth of the theory of evolution does not make it true. Hence to take one's stand in the "reason" of the day is specious "reasoning". But what if reason is taken in the sense that Hodge gave above? What if reason is the laws of thought, those laws necessary for thought itself? Hodge saw the law of non-contradiction as an obvious example. While VanTil argued that only Christian Theism can explain such a law, it seems he nevertheless used the law to argue for theism. His Transcendental Argument presupposes the law of non-contradiction. The non-Christian world and life view is false because it is self-contradictory, therefore Christianity is true. This is the law of non-contradiction being applied to basic beliefs. Therefore, it seems that the first assumption is that this law is necessary for thought, and only after that does one question which view is consistent.

What does this say for clarity? VanTil both affirmed general revelation, and the necessity of the Scriptures for any knowledge. This is not the distinction that both Warfield and Kuyper made above with respect to the work of the Holy Spirit to renew men's hearts. VanTil agreed with them on that issue. But his use of Scripture as the presupposition necessary for all knowledge is more than this; it is an epistemological claim about how to know, not an ontological claim about the ability to know. For VanTil the fall of man was when man tried to do without God in every part of life.[24] Humans sought the source of truth, goodness, and beauty in something besides God, either in self or in the material universe. The result is that humans tried to establish a worldview in which he interpreted all data apart from reference to God. In contrast VanTil argued that persons must take their ideas about the nature of reality from the Bible. The final standard of truth itself is the Bible. This is importantly different than Warfield. Remember that Warfield argued that the Bible must first be authenticated as special revelation. This means that for Warfield there is a standard for gaining knowledge more basic than the Bible itself.

VanTil affirmed what was said about the relation of redemptive revelation (supernatural revelation, or Scriptures), and general revelation (natural revelation). He argued that special revelation is necessary because of the covenant disobedience on the part of Adam in paradise.[25] VanTil saw the sin that caused humanity to fall as a violation of a positive supernatural revelation. That is, God spoke to Adam and told him not to eat of the tree. What VanTil left unclear is how Adam knew it was God that told him this. How did Adam know God? Presumably one must first know God before one can know not to violate a command of God. It seems at least fair to assert that it was first a failure to know God as the Creator that allowed Adam to eat and break God's command. This knowing God as Creator is what all humans are held accountable for. But VanTil's description of the fall as only the breaking of a commandment leaves unclear for what humanity is held accountable.

If the above considerations are correct, it follows that humanity could know God apart from the Christian Scriptures. Perhaps, aspects of God's justice, mercy, and redemption could not be known and are properly the subject of redemptive revelation, but God's eternal power and divine nature could be known. And it follows that these can be known of God after the fall through general revelation: reason does not fall (as if the law of non-contradiction became false after the fall), but rather the desire to use reason changed. VanTil maintained that these truths about God can be known even after the fall.[26] "Grace can be recognized as grace only in contrast to God's curse on nature."[27] In this VanTil agrees with the Westminster Confession in stating that all creation is a revelation of the nature of God, and it is in this light that Scriptures as redemptive revelation make sense. But if God can be known through general revelation and yet all knowledge is through the Bible there appears to be a discrepancy.

VanTil's remedy for this difficulty was to claim that fallen men do in fact know God. It is not just that it is clear that God exists so that if men thought about it, if they cared to use reason, they could know. It is the case that this knowledge actually gets through to those in the fallen condition. That this was VanTil's view makes sense of his idea of the fall as a particular violation of a command. Adam already knew God. The problem was in Adam's attitude, or heart. Not only are the invisible things of God displayed all around man, as well as in him, they actually "get through."[28] VanTil gave as evidences of this fact the self-conscious activity of a person, a person's negative moral reaction to the revelation around him, a person's sense of dissatisfaction with all non-theistic interpretations, and the measure of involuntary recognition of the truth of the theistic interpretation as the true interpretation of the world. VanTil argued that these show that general revelation is known by all men.

Rather than solve the problem this solution presents more problems. VanTil claimed that the knowledge of God is clear because men already know it. It is necessarily known. "The *intelligibility of anything, for man, presupposes the existence of God* - the God whose nature and character are delineated in God's revelation, found both in nature and in Scripture. It is this God - the only God - whom all men of necessity, 'know'."[29] According to VanTil, the fallen humans "suppress" what they know in the sense of both knowing and trying not to know at the same time. This places the problem not as a problem of knowledge, but as a problem of desire. This creates a strange kind of person that both knows God as the source of all things good, and does not want what is good.[30] One is reminded of Satan as portrayed in Milton's paradise lost. In this work Satan rebels against God and God's view of the good and says, "evil be thou my good."[31] Satan is still seeking what he thinks is good, he simply disagrees with the statement "God is good." It seems then that a person in this state actually has a difference of opinion over what is good, and hence they disagree ultimately with the claim that God is good. Does such a person know God? Certainly part of knowing God is knowing that God is good. Insofar as someone fails to know this of God, they are failing to know God. The sense in which all men know God is therefore left highly ambiguous.

VanTil's view of clarity therefore seems to have some significant difficulties that spring from his view of inexcusability. For VanTil humans are inexcusable for not acting on what they already know, rather than for failing to know what they should know (unbelief).

The operative assumption throughout this work is that guilt assumes inexcusability. Humans are guilty for not having known what is clear about God. If humans have known this even in their fallen state, then what is it that they are guilty of? If it is that they have not given to God the worship due Him, then this seems to follow from their not recognizing God as God (the Creator). This seems to be a lack of knowledge that results in wrong action. VanTil affirmed that general revelation is sufficient:

> After the fall of man natural revelation is still historically sufficient. It is sufficient for such as have in Adam brought the curse of God upon nature. It is sufficient to render them without excuse.[32]

It is sufficient to hold humans inexcusable. But what exactly is enough for that? The Apostle Paul seems to affirm that it is more than a bare knowledge of God, but instead that it is a knowledge of God's eternal power and divine nature (much more than a mere "higher power"). General revelation is enough to give that knowledge. VanTil claimed that the Triune God is necessary for all knowledge. For VanTil it is not that theism is one worldview among many that might have some truths. It is that apart from theism no knowledge is possible at all. Wesley A Roberts said that according to VanTil the most basic of all facts is the existence of the triune God.[33] The existence of the triune God is not simply reasonable or probably true, it is a necessary presupposition for any other belief. Consequently, VanTil held that unless a person believes in the triune God of the Bible, no other belief could be logically supported.

In taking this position VanTil affirmed logic. Either believe in God or lose intelligibility. The assumption is that one would want a logical worldview. This seems like a safe assumption, especially if logic is taken in the narrow sense as the laws of inference. Again, here the law of non-contradiction shows up. Is it that all non-Christian worldviews violate this law, while Christianity does not? If so, then it seems that this law is necessary for knowledge. Or is it that only theism provides us with the possibility of such a law, and therefore theism is necessary for knowledge? Should reason be assumed in order to find the correct worldview, or should theism be assumed in order to establish reason? The latter appears to beg the question in that it assumes the law is desirable, and then uses it to show that all non-Christian views violate it. The former is free from such problems, and appears to be what the Hodges and Warfield were affirming. In answering the question "how do I know" it is necessary to proceed from epistemology (reason) to ontology (the nature of being).

However, VanTil continued from this point to argue that it is the Scriptures that are necessary for any knowledge. While Warfield argued that one must first have the Scriptures proven as such, VanTil saw this as holding God to human standards of knowledge where God is the author of knowledge. It is certainly true that many people have rejected the Scriptures for less than adequate "reasons." But this does not mean that the law of non-contradiction is an arbitrary standard invented by humans. VanTil believed that if anything is to be intelligible or coherent, it must be based on the truth of the Christian Scriptures.[34] This is based on VanTil's view of Christ as the source of knowledge itself. The Apostle John speaks of Christ this way in John chapter 1. VanTil took the *logos* spoken of in John to refer to Christ and the Scriptures, while others, like Gordon Clark[35] argued that *logos* should also be taken to refer to logic and hence the "word" is what illuminates men's minds even with respect to general revelation. But for VanTil the standard is the Bible itself.[36] It seems wrong to say that Warfield appealed to a non-Christian standard when speaking of "right reason" in that Warfield claimed right reason necessarily reveals God, and is therefore by no means a non-Christian standard.

However, it should be noted that VanTil did not argue that one must go to the Scriptures for all kinds of knowledge. He explicitly said otherwise. He argued that there is nothing in the universe about which humans can have a full understanding unless the Bible is taken into account. This does not mean that a person should consult the Bible rather than the laboratory in order to understand the anatomy of a snake. But if a person only goes to the laboratory then he/she will not have a full understanding, or even a true interpretation, of the snake. According to VanTil, this reality makes it necessary for apologetics to have a definitely assigned place in the orthodox seminary.[37]

What VanTil said is that the knowledge of God derived from the Scriptures is necessary for any other knowledge because it is the basic presupposition on which all else is founded. The question therefore remains: if the Scriptures are necessary for a coherent world and life view, to what extent is general revelation enough to hold men inexcusable? If the Scriptures are a redemptive revelation designed to explain how God will return humanity to the truth, then that truth must be available in the first place in order for a return to it to be a coherent notion. If general revelation reveals the eternal power and divine nature of God, then this is not a bare "higher power" but a full knowledge. Thus, general revelation is not simply a bare minimum.

VanTil viewed Warfield's system of apologetics as involving a stress on the objective, intelligible, and clear revelation of God to all humans.[38] This revelation is so objectively clear that it is not rational to reject the Christian faith. VanTil concurred with this part of Warfield's view. For Warfield there was ideally only one science, and Christianity is the only intelligible system of truth. VanTil criticized Warfield, however, because he saw Warfield's system as only providing "probability" rather than necessity. VanTil's principal argument was to show the absurdity of the contradiction. If the opposite is impossible then Christianity must be true (this is the use of the law of non-contradiction). In essence VanTil characterized Warfield as an evidentialist. There are aspects of Warfield's approach that can be characterized as evidentialist. Such an approach only establishes the probability of the Christian worldview and not the inexcusability of unbelief. VanTil maintained that Warfield argued for the probability of Christianity's truth. VanTil also argued that while there is only one science, those engaged in the scientific endeavor are subjectively and spiritually at war in their principles and goals. For VanTil the only way an unbeliever can contribute to the body of science is by departing from their principles and presuppositions. VanTil's emphasis was that on the natural man's principles nothing would be intelligible at all.[39]

It could be true that while Warfield provides the foundation for clarity and inexcusability, he did not develop this and remained content with probability. But does VanTil provide a framework for clarity and inexcusability? Just like Kuyper, VanTil held that the materialist worldview is the opposite of Christianity. Many of his arguments are directed against materialism. But if materialism is false, does this mean theism is true? Did not Plato also argue against materialism with his dualism? And spiritual monists also argue against materialism. While VanTil's method is sound (if the opposite is impossible Christianity is true), it is vitally important that this method find the real opposite, not a contrary.

Kuyper, on the other hand, avoided evidentialism with a view, as noted above, that can be called worldview relativism. VanTil saw Kuyper's main contribution as delineating that there are two basic principles at work, each of which produces a different worldview and hence two different "sciences." This was what VanTil saw as Kuyper's "distinctive and masterful insight into apologetics."[40] The two conflicting principles that are at work in the believer and unbeliever (God versus autonomy) result in two opposing theories of knowledge.[41] The alienation from God due to sin has a significant impact on the natural man, in contrast to the enlightening work of the Holy Spirit in the regenerated man's mind.[42] VanTil agreed with Kuyper in maintaining that there is a different orientation in terms of attitude, or heart, that results in different lifestyles.[43] This is somewhat different than Warfield in that Warfield saw the difference with respect to the use of reason, not with respect to an attitude.

However, VanTil criticized Kuyper in his view of apologetics. Kuyper concluded that apologetics is essentially useless. VanTil saw this as a mistake in Kuyper, being inferred from the antithesis between belief and unbelief and the resulting two sciences.[44] For Kuyper there was little use for reasoning with the unbeliever since the unbeliever disagrees as to what makes a "reasonable" argument. VanTil thought that Kuyper stumbled at this point in that God has clearly revealed Himself in nature and history so that the unbeliever is not doing justice to the objective facts when he does not submit to God as his Creator. And the unbeliever never ceases to be made in the image of God, and so it is only in thinking God's thoughts after him that a person can find an intelligible foundation for knowledge and experience.[45]

VanTil affirmed that there is a clear revelation of God in nature and history and that the unbeliever must deny this in order to hold his fallen worldview. Thus, apologetics has the task of showing the unbeliever that his world and life view is incoherent. However VanTil saw in Kuyper something that made him take Kuyper's position. He found it impossible to hold with Kuyper that because of the difference between the Christian and the non-Christian worldviews it is useless for the Christian to reason with the non-Christian. But he viewed Warfield as asserting that the difference is only one of degree, which he also found unacceptable. And so he took the position of Kuyper without taking the position that reasoning between the Christian and the non-Christian is useless.[46] This seems to imply that there is a common basis for reasoning, or something that both the Christian and the non-Christian would accept as reason.

Greg Bahnsen argued that VanTil drew the best insights from Warfield and Kuyper and formed them into a transcendental, presuppositional apologetic that defeats all philosophical challenges to the Biblical worldview.[47] VanTil did find something beneficial in both Warfield and Kuyper, and he stated this when he said that Warfield was correct in claiming that Christianity is objectively defensible, and that the natural man has the ability to understand. The natural man must be shown that on his own principles all truth and meaning is lost.[48] VanTil also argued, and this is part of the problem in his view of man mentioned above, that the unbeliever can understand Christianity intellectually while not understanding it spiritually.[49]

Even so, VanTil's analysis seems to leave some problems. Did Warfield really only allow for the probability of the truth of Christianity? Warfield said "without the knowledge of God it is not too much to say we know nothing rightly, so that the renunciation of the knowledge of God carries with it renunciation of all right knowledge."[50] That Warfield believed this seems contrary to how VanTil portrayed him. If Warfield followed Charles Hodge, and Hodge was arguing from the law of non-contradiction to the incoherence of all non-Christian views, does this really allow for the possibility that one of them is true? If Warfield's position was that there is a right reason that is necessary for thought itself, and this reason reveals the eternal power and divine nature of God, then this seems to imply that reason leads only to belief in God. This establishes a foundation on which it can be argued that there is a clear general revelation of God's existence to all humans and that therefore unbelief is inexcusable and leaves humanity in need of redemption.

Similarly, VanTil's view of Kuyper presents some problems. If there are two worldviews, as Kuyper said, then it seems that both of them will claim that the other is incorrect (based on some standard that the other does not accept). Hence to say that the fallen worldview is incorrect because it is self-contradictory is simply to continue to affirm one's own presupposition. What is necessary is that there is rationality, which serves as a common ground for all humans, and reveals the existence of God. This is the method of apologetics, and, as Warfield said, there is only one science with a number of incorrect attempts at it. In this case reason stands as the necessary precondition for thought. If the fallen worldview violates reason, then it is incoherent. This is certainly different from saying that only the theistic position allows for reason, which is what it seems VanTil tried to maintain.

Given the above considerations, VanTil's position uses circular reasoning. VanTil asked: "If it is true that the difference between Christian and anti-theistic epistemology is as fundamental as we have contended that it is, and if it is true that the antitheist takes his position for granted at the outset of his investigations, and if it is true that the Christian expects his opponent to do nothing else in as much as according to Scripture the 'natural man' cannot discern the things of the Spirit, we must ask *whether* it is then of any use for the Christian to reason with his opponent".[51] His answer was that the message must not be toned down by arguing that epistemological terminology means the same thing for theists and non-theists alike. There is almost always a difference when unbelievers use the term "reason" in contrast to when believers use the term "reason." Instead, the answer must be found in the concept of Christian theism, where God only is absolute. It does not seem that Warfield would have disagreed with this conclusion. Certainly Warfield would have agreed that God only is absolute. That there is a "right reason" by which humanity comes to know God does not subordinate God to reason.

In this sense all worldviews are circular in that all worldviews have assumptions. However, this does not mean that all assumptions are coherent. And it means that if an assumption/presupposition is incoherent, it is so because of some standard of thought that applies to all presuppositions. VanTil affirmed God as absolute, Darwin/Marx/Freud affirm matter as such, Plato the forms, etc. How can a person decide which presupposition to take for themselves? If there is no method of deciding that is objective to all, then persons cannot be held accountable for making the "correct" decision. However, if there is such a method, then it is not the product of one of them but stands as judge over all. To argue that the Christian epistemology is the best, and that Christianity is necessary for this epistemology, is simply not an argument. Marx and Plato each say the same of their worldview. There appears to be a sense then in which reason, as the laws of thought, as what Reid was looking for, as the law of non-contradiction identified by Charles Hodge and Warfield, is transcendental. Reason is necessary for argumentation and hence cannot be argued against. While some people might try to argue against such laws, in their arguments they are assuming these laws and hence displaying their own inconsistency. VanTil's approach, showing the impossibility of the contradiction of Christianity, is a sound approach. However, it is reason that shows contradictions, not an affirmation of the existence of God. The latter is exactly what must be proven. If the proof is the transcendental proof argued for by VanTil (that God must be assumed to have any intelligibility at all), this seems to be coherent (provide meaning) only because the laws of identity, excluded middle, and non-contradiction are used to argue for the necessity of God. God is necessary for intelligibility because all other worldviews violate the law of non-contradiction and hence violate reason. In the most basic sense reason is necessary for intelligibility. Not all worldview presuppositions are coherent.

VanTil, as one of the prominent thinkers in Warfield's legacy, does contribute by expounding the notion of the transcendental argument and the necessity of realizing one's presuppositions. However, his explanation of inexcusability, clarity, and how God is known, has enough problems to make his apologetic approach suffer and become problematically circular. Inexcusability requires not circularity but the use of reason to establish one's presupposition. Reason, as the laws of thought, should not be confused with a presupposition because reason, as the laws of thought, is used for establishing any meaningful presupposition.

Notes

1. Reid, W. Stanford, "J. Gresham Machen," in *Reformed Theology in America*, ed. David Wells (Grand Rapids: Baker Books, 1997) 97.
2. Reid, "J. Gresham Machen," 97.
3. VanTil, Cornelius, *Christian Apologetics* (Phillipsburg: Presbyterian and Reformed Publishing, 1976), 1.
4. VanTil, *Christian*, 1.
5. VanTil, *Christian*, 1.
6. VanTil, *Christian*, 2.
7. Bahnsen, Greg L, *VanTil's Apologetic: Readings and Analysis* (Phillipsburg: Presbyterian and Reformed Publishing, 1998), 30.
8. Bahnsen, *VanTil's*, 30.
9. Kant, Immanuel, "Critique of Pure Reason," in *Modern Philosophy*, ed. Forrest E. Baird and Walter Kaufmann (Prentice Hall, New Jersey: 1997), 491-531. 510.
10. Fuller, "Reformed," 92.
11. Fuller, "Reformed," 91.
12. Bahnsen, *VanTil's*, 30.
13. Bahnsen, *VanTil's*, 30.
14. VanTil, *Christian*, 10.
15. VanTil, *Christian*, 96.
16. Bahnsen, *VanTil's*, 30.
17. Bahnsen, *VanTil's*, 61.
18. Bahnsen, *VanTil's*, 61.
19. Bahnsen, *VanTil's*, 6.
20. Bahnsen, *VanTil's*, 6.
21. Bahnsen, *VanTil's*, 6.
22. Bahnsen, *VanTil's*, 6.
23. Bahnsen, *VanTil's*, 6.
24. Note that while Warfield, in contrast to VanTil, held that right reason can arrive at the knowledge of God revealed in the creation, he did say "With the fullest recognition of the validity of all the knowledge of God and His ways with men, which can be obtained through the manifestations of His power and divinity in nature and history and grace; and the frankest allowance that the written Word is given, not to destroy the manifestations of God, but to fulfill them; the theologian must yet refuse to give these sources of knowledge a place alongside of the written Word" (Idea 61).
25. Bahnsen, *VanTil's*, 95.
26. VanTil, *Christian*, 30.
27. VanTil, *Christian*, 31.
28. VanTil, *Christian*, 31.
29. Bahnsen, *VanTil's*, 187.
30. Bahnsen, *VanTil's*, 192.
31. Helseth argues that Princeton's affirmation of the soul as a single unit implies a connection between knowing, feeling, and willing (Helseth, "B.B. Warfield," 157).
32. Milton, John, *Paradise Lost* (Chicago: Encyclopedia Britannica, 1948), 154.
33. VanTil, *Christian*, 33.
34. Roberts, Wesley A, "Cornelius VanTil," in *Reformed Theology in America* ed. David Wells (Grand Rapids: Baker Books, 1997), 175.
35. Bahnsen, *VanTil's*, 6.
36. Clark is mentioned here because of his strong Reformed heritage and his opposition to VanTil. For more on the debate between Clark and VanTil read: *The Clark-VanTil Controversy* by Herman Hoeksema.

37. Bahnsen, *VanTil's*, 95.
38. VanTil, *Christian*, 2.
39. Bahnsen, *VanTil's*, 597.
40. Bahnsen, *VanTil's*, 598.
41. Bahnsen, *VanTil's*, 598.
42. Bahnsen, *VanTil's*, 598.
43. Bahnsen, *VanTil's*, 598.
44. Bahnsen, *VanTil's*, 598.
45. Bahnsen, *VanTil's*, 599.
46. Bahnsen, *VanTil's*, 599.
47. Bahnsen, *VanTil's*, 601.
48. Bahnsen, *VanTil's*, 600.
49. Bahnsen, *VanTil's*, 608.Bahnsen, *VanTil's*, 608.
50. Warfield, *Studies*, 97.
51. VanTil, Cornelius. *A Survey of Christian Epistemology* (Phillipsburg: Presbyterian and Reformed Publishing), x.

## Conclusion:

This book has examined B.B. Warfield's view of apologetics, his context at Princeton, his debate with Kuyper, and his legacy at Westminster Theological Seminary. The assumptions concerning inexcusability, clarity, and rationality that are behind Warfield's apologetic were examined in order to bring his view into focus and contrast it with Kuyper and VanTil. Warfield's view of right reason provides apologetics with the necessary components of inexcusability and clarity. In contrast, the systems of both Kuyper and VanTil do not explain the need for clarity and rationality to establish inexcusability and therefore minimize the role of apologetics and bring rationality itself into question. While there are aspects of Warfield's system that may need closer attention, or even parts that appear problematic, his affirmation of right reason and the ability for all persons at all times to know God makes sense of inexcusability and redemption in a way that other systems do not. If there are failings in Warfield's view it is particularly with respect to being underdeveloped in these areas.

The focus has been on the knowledge of God because of the Christian claim that the failure to know God is inexcusable. However, this book has not looked at Warfield's actual proofs for God's existence. It makes sense to conclude by giving a brief summary of Warfield's view of the knowledge of God and consider some possible problems and questions remaining to be answered. Of the knowledge of God's existence Warfield said that there is an intuitive knowledge of God which is both universal and unavoidable.[1] This truth is given in the very same act as the idea of self, because the self is dependent and implies one on whom it is dependent. This immediate perception of God is supported by the theistic proofs.[2] These proofs give us not only God's existence but also his nature as a personal Spirit, who is infinite and eternal, and having properties such as power, knowledge, wisdom, righteousness, holiness, goodness.[3]

## Conclusion

There are three possible problems in Warfield's approach to the knowledge of God. First, the idea of God's existence as an intuitive truth is unclear and ultimately not helpful in establishing inexcusability. Second, his reliance on the theistic proofs in light of substantial challenges to these raised by David Hume and Immanuel Kant. Third, whether this approach, often called evidentialism, can provide certainty or only probability.

The idea of an intuitive knowledge of God, an immediate knowledge of God, or the *sensus divinitatus*, is the claim that everybody has some knowledge of God naturally and unavoidably. Unbelief is thus viewed as an attempt to avoid what is unavoidable. Those who hold this position sometimes tell non-theists that they really do believe in God but are not acknowledging this belief. The problem with this is that the knowledge that everyone is supposed to have of God is either not universal, or extremely vague. It is easy to prove that not everybody has a knowledge or belief in God as defined by theism (a spirit, infinite, eternal, and unchanging in power, knowledge, goodness, etc.). It does not follow that because humans are dependent on another being that this other being is God in the theistic sense of that term. Theistic belief has not been held by every human throughout history, nor is it held by every human alive today. To assert that the *sensus divinitatus* is a much more general knowing of God, more like a higher power or greater other, is to concede that the idea of God is not known intuitively because God is not merely a higher power or greater other. Nor is it sufficient to affirm that all humans have worshiped something and that this "something" counts as the *sensus divinitatus*. The actual object of worship, say Zeus, Baal, Thor, et. al., is very different from God. And yet Romans 1:20 affirms that God's eternal power and divine nature are knowable so that ignorance of these is inexcusable.

It is the eternal power and divine nature of God that Paul says is knowable and the ignorance of which is inexcusable (Romans 1:20), not a vague sense of a higher power. And when Paul says that God's existence and nature are known *from* the things that are made this suggests an inference, not an immediate or intuitive truth. When Paul says in verse 21 that "although they knew God, they did not glorify Him as God, nor were thankful, but became futile in their thoughts, and their foolish hearts were darkened" (NKJV) there seems to be a progression from having known God to failing to know God. It is far from clear that the word "they" in this passage refers to all humans who have ever lived, but rather may be referring to an original context where humans knew God, and then a process wherein humanity exchanged belief in God for belief in idols.

Further, non-theists can make a similar claim about their belief. It is easy to assert that "deep down" everyone really believes the truth. The problem with such a claim for Christianity is that it does not maintain that unbelief is inexcusable because there is no unbelief since everyone beliefs intuitively. But the inexcusability of unbelief, of the failure to know God's eternal power and divine nature from the things that have been made, is a central part of Romans 1. In terms of Old Princeton and Warfield the claim that God's existence is known intuitively may be an effect of Reid's Common Sense Philosophy. As was noted in Chapter 1, many of the truths that this philosophy claims are known through common sense are in fact disputed and require proof. God's existence is one such example. A related claim is that a person is within his/her "epistemic rights" to believe in God without proof. This is a different claim altogether than that all humans have an intuitive idea of God, although both may have been influenced by Reid. To establish that a given person is within his/her epistemic rights does not establish that unbelief is inexcusable and requires redemption through Christ. To maintain that unbelief requires redemption it is necessary to establish that unbelief is inexcusable.

A second problem in Warfield's method is that he, and Old School Princeton more generally, tended toward evidentialism. He seems to have taken this approach to establishing the veracity of the Bible. "This method, as we have seen, seeks to build upon the basis of adequate evidence *grounds* for the validity of the Christian faith prior to personal commitment."[4] Robert Reymond sees this method present in Warfield in the latter's argument for the inspiration of the Bible. Warfield said:

> We do not adopt the doctrine of the plenary inspiration of Scripture on sentimental grounds, nor even, as we have already had occasion to remark, on *a priori* or general grounds of whatever kind. We adopt it specifically because it is taught us as truth by Christ and His apostles, in the Scriptural record of their teaching, and the evidence for its truth is, therefore, as we have also already pointed out, precisely that evidence, in weight and amount, which vindicates for us the trustworthiness of Christ and His apostles as teachers of doctrine. Of course, this evidence is not in the strict logical sense "demonstrative;"

it is "probable" evidence. It therefore leaves open the metaphysical possibility of its being mistaken.[5]

Probability does not establish inexcusability. If the Bible could be mistaken, then unbelief cannot be said to be inexcusable. There is an excuse for not believing, namely, that a person believes one of the other alternatives that might be correct if the Bible is mistaken. "But evidence, at best, is *only probable* and, at worst, *meaningless* in the natural man's world where Chance is ultimate. . . . The evidentialist himself admits his case is *at best* a probable one. This approach leaves the man who refuses to regard the evidence as compelling with the delusion that the *best* basis the Christian can claim for his faith is a probable one."[6]

Both Kuyper and VanTil saw the problems in the evidential approach. They saw that what counts as evidence in one worldview may not count as evidence in another worldview. As was seen in previous chapters their response was to assert that there is not neutral ground between the Christian and the non-Christian worldviews. What is evidence for the Christian will not count as evidence for the non-Christian. This is a very helpful insight, and it may be that Warfield failed to see this in using an evidentialist approach.

However, it is not clear that Warfield asserted that all aspects of the Christian worldview are only established on probability through the use of evidence. He does not seem to approach God's existence this way. He speaks of the necessity of belief in God, and that this can be established through proofs.[7] Perhaps there is a tension in Warfield on this point. His approach to God's existence appears to support the claim in Romans that unbelief is inexcusable. He affirms that reason is common ground for all humans, although it is not neutral because it leads to theism and finds a contradiction in non-theism. But something can be taken from Kuyper and VanTil by seeing that worldviews are logical systems that are proven or refuted by addressing their internal consistency, and the consistency of the presuppositions from which the entire worldview is derived. What must be established by apologetics is the inexcusability of non-theism as a worldview (or multiple different worldviews). Warfield affirms this can be done with respect to the existence of God, and perhaps it is left to others to take it further.

Finally, problems may arise for Warfield's method due to his reliance on the theistic proofs. These proofs received an important challenge by both David Hume and Immanuel Kant. This challenge has led many to conclude that God's existence cannot be proven. Kant's challenge is directed at all proof of God's existence, which he asserts ultimately rests on the ontological proof. "Thus the physico-theological proof [teleological proof] of the existence of an original or supreme being rests upon the cosmological proof, and the cosmological upon the ontological. And since, besides these three, there is no other path open to speculative reason, the ontological proof from pure concepts of reason is the only possible one, if indeed any proof of a proposition so far exalted above all empirical employment of the understanding is possible at all."[8] And the ontological proof, according to Kant, does not prove the existence of God.

> The concept of a supreme being is in many respects a very useful idea; but just because it is a mere idea, it is altogether incapable, by itself alone, of enlarging our knowledge in regard to what exists. . . . The attempt to establish the existence of a supreme being by means of the famous ontological argument of Descartes is therefore merely so much labour and effort lost; we can no more extend our stock of [theoretical] insight by mere ideas, than a merchant can better his position by adding a few noughts to his cash account.[9]

The central challenge present in Kant appears to be a challenge to reason and then to the theistic proofs. For such proofs to be successful reason must be able to tell us about existence. If it cannot do so, then the theistic proofs, and any proofs about what exists apart from sense experience, are unsound. This is an important challenge that must be addressed if theistic proofs are to be successful. It requires an examination and clarification about the nature of reason, especially in its ontological function in applying to both thought and being.

In his debate with Kuyper over apologetics, Warfield affirmed the necessity of establishing God's existence through rational argument in order to make sense of the Christian worldview. The claim that humans need redemption through Christ for their unbelief presupposes that unbelief is inexcusable. The purpose of this book has been to argue for the necessity of the inexcusability of unbelief within the Christian worldview, and argue that Warfield's approach to apologetics preserves this, in contrast to Kuyper and VanTil. However, it has also been seen that there is in Warfield a problem in his claim about intuitive knowledge of God, a possible tension due to evidentialist aspects of his approach, and more work to be done on the theistic proofs. This gives direction for further work in the area of apologetics and the question of the inexcusability of unbelief.

Notes

1. Warfield, Studies in Theology, 110.
2. Warfield, Studies in Theology, 110.
3. Warfield, Studies in Theology, 110.
4. Robert L. Reymond. *The Justification of Knowledge: An Introductory Study of Christian Apologetic Methodology*. Presbyterian and Reformed Publishing Company, 1976. 61.
5. Benjamin B. Warfield, "The Real Problem of Inspiration" in *Revelation and Inspiration*. Baker Book House, Grand Rapids, 2000. (218).
6. Reymond, *Justification*, 67.
7. Warfield, *Studies*, 110.
8. Immanuel Kant. "Critique of Theistic Proofs" in *Classical and Contemporary Readings in the Philosophy of Religion*, ed. John Hick, Prentice Hall, Upper Saddle River, 1990. 140.
9. Kant, *Critique*, 126.

www.ingramcontent.com/pod-product-compliance
Lightning Source LLC
Chambersburg PA
CBHW021134300426
44113CB00006B/421